FOR LIFE-GIVING LEADERS

THE ART OF TRANSFORMATIONAL LEADERSHIP

HABITUDES®

IMAGES
THAT FORM
LEADERSHIP
HABITS &
ATTITUDES

BY
DR TIM
ELMORE

Published in Atlanta, Georgia by Growing Leaders, Inc. (www.GrowingLeaders.com)

ISBN: 978-1-7320703-2-5

Printed in the United States of America

Library of Congress Cataloguing-in-Publication Data

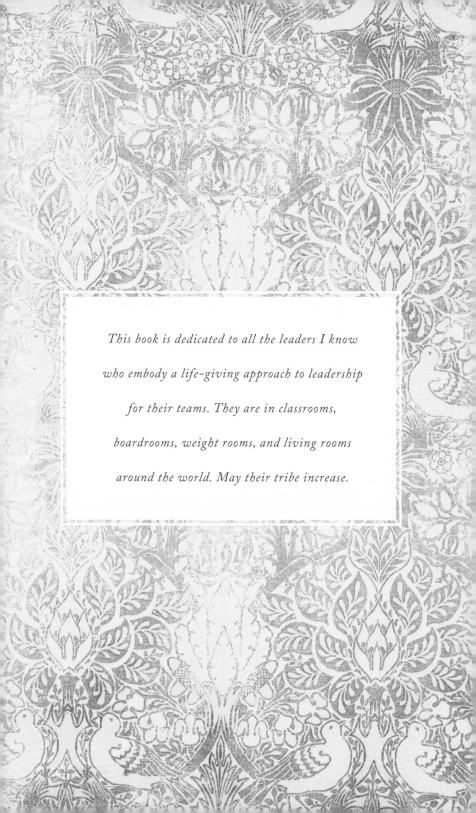

This book is dedicated to all the leaders I know

who embody a life-giving approach to leadership

for their teams. They are in classrooms,

boardrooms, weight rooms, and living rooms

around the world. May their tribe increase.

TABLE OF CONTENTS

★

A WORD ABOUT IMAGES

We live in a culture rich with images. We grew up with photographs, TV, movies, video, MTV and DVDs. We can't escape the power of the visual image—and most of us don't want to.

I've learned over my career that most of us are visual learners. We like to see a picture, not just hear a word. Author Leonard Sweet says that images are the language of the 21st century, not words. Some of the best communicators in history taught using the power of the metaphor and image—from Jesus Christ and His parables to Martin Luther King Jr. and his "I Have a Dream" speech, during the Civil Rights movement. "The best leaders," writes Tom Peters, "…almost without exception and at every level, are master users of stories and symbols."

Why? Because pictures stick. We remember pictures long after words have left us. When we hear a speech, we often remember the stories from that speech, more than the phrases used by the speaker, because they painted a picture inside of us. They communicate far more than mere words. In fact, words are helpful only as they conjure up a picture in our minds. Most of us think in pictures. If I say the word "elephant" to you, you don't picture the letters: e-l-e-p-h-a-n-t. You picture a big gray animal. Pictures are what we file away in our minds. They enable us to store huge volumes of information. There's an old phrase that has stood the test of time: A picture is worth a thousand words. I believe it's true. While studying commercial art in college I recognized the power of the image. Now I get to combine the power of teaching leadership truths with the power of pictures. I hope they linger in your mind and heart. I hope you discover layers of reality in them, as you grow in your leadership skills. I trust they'll impact you profoundly as they have me.

This Particular Book

The purpose of this particular resource is to offer you a picture of what I believe a leader should look like as they fully mature. Its very different than the image we frequently see in leaders today who seek power and count "likes" and "views" on social media. In contrast, this leader is life-giving. Life-giving leaders are all about people and causes that are outside of themselves. The book illustrates a new kind of leader's lifestyle. While it contains both life-giving habits and attitudes—much of this book is about a leader's approach and attitudes about what it means to influence a team of people.

I believe the best leaders are not merely transactional in nature. They are transformational. They breathe life on others, inspiring them to perform in a better way than they could have without that leader. A life-giving leader brings out the best in people by believing the best about people.

They take the high road and influence others to do the same. They change the culture of the organization or team they lead because of the way they carry themselves and by the way they interact with their team.

- THEY INSPIRE
- THEY BELIEVE
- THEY LISTEN
- THEY STRENGTHEN
- THEY MOTIVATE
- THEY EMPOWER

Some sociologists describe this generation as EPIC: Experiential, Participatory, Image-driven and Connected. If that's true, I believe we'll get the most out of resources that give us an image, an experience and a way to connect with each other. Each of these books provides you not only with an image, but a handful of stories, questions, a self-assessment and an exercise in which you can participate. Dive in and experience each one of them. My hope is that they become signposts that guide you, and warn you and inform you on your leadership journey.

Dr. Tim Elmore

Quarterbacks and Referees

ALL FOOTBALL GAMES HAVE QUARTERBACKS WHO PROVIDE DIRECTION, INSPIRE AND DEPLOY THE TEAM. THE REFEREES ARE THERE TO ENFORCE THE RULES OF THE GAME, WATCH THE BOUNDARIES AND CALL FOULS. NO ONE ATTENDS A FOOTBALL GAME TO SEE A REFEREE. LIFE-GIVING LEADERS FIGHT THE TENDENCY TO MERELY REFEREE. THEY ARE THE QUARTERBACKS.

I love watching college and professional football. Because our organization, Growing Leaders, serves so many teams in the NCAA and NFL, I get the chance to meet coaches and players from all over the country and watch plenty of games.

After recently witnessing an incredible game, I started thinking about what attracted me so much to this sport. It's a potent combination of strength and strategy. It's about managing the clock, blending the talent on a team, and using every tool available to your advantage. In fact, it's very difficult to win consistently without good leadership on a football team.

It dawned on me that every competition actually has two leaders on the field who are essential to the flow and the outcome of the game, yet we rarely compare them. There is one that we want to watch and one we don't pay much attention to: the quarterback and the referee.

TWO KINDS OF LEADERS IN FOOTBALL

If you think about it, referees are essential because the results of so many plays on the gridiron are debatable. We need those folks with the striped shirts to watch each play closely and blow the whistle when they believe it's over. Especially on close plays, both teams trust referees to maintain order on the field. Without referees who would decide if a pass is incomplete? Who would prevent a late hit? How would we know if the running back breaks the plain and scores a touchdown? In many ways, referees offer a necessary piece of leadership that protects the integrity of the game.

Quarterbacks are a much different kind of leader. The good ones are incredible to watch. They are smart, agile, and can see everything on the field (much like a good referee). But, quarterbacks are all about moving the ball toward the end zone: passing, running, or handing it off so their team can score. Over a career, good quarterbacks display how important it is to leverage the talent around them to win. The great quarterbacks like Joe Namath, Roger Staubach, Joe Montana, Troy Aikman, John Elway, Peyton Manning, Tom Brady, or Cam Newton make everyone around them perform better.

When I pause to reflect, it's clear the game needs both quarterbacks and referees. But, there's a big difference. A referee is not central to the meaning of the game. No one ever attends a football game to watch the referee.

LESSONS FROM THE PLAYING FIELD

As I've watched leaders over the years, I have noticed a pattern. We often begin our careers like a quarterback: we're inspiring, we've got ideas, we have the vision to make progress for our organization. Over time, however, we often begin to look more like a referee. Our work becomes more about calling people out when we believe they're out of bounds or blowing the whistle when we see something wrong. When our focus in life becomes more about compliance to rules than accomplishing a mission, we might as well put on a striped shirt.

This comparison of the referee and the quarterback is too important to miss. The shift we make from relationships to regulations can be both subtle and frightening. Life-giving leaders are entrepreneurial and, therefore, very attractive. Even when their organization is well established, they remain innovative and passionate. Sadly, too many leaders spiral into a lifeless routine of officiating within a few years. They can even become repulsive. Note the contrast below:

REFEREES	QUARTERBACKS
1. Calling penalties	1. Making progress
2. Information	2. Inspiration
3. Counting players on the field	3. Empowering players on the field
4. All about downs and rules	4. All about delegation and results
5. Keeping the ball in bounds	5. Moving the ball forward
6. Aim is to control the plays	6. Aim is to connect with players
7. The goal is maintenance	7. The goal is the mission

My friend, Steven, is a great example of this shift. He launched a company right out of college and labored tirelessly out of passion for the new products and services he'd created. After eight years, he took his company public. Soon, he assumed larger managerial roles and gained the respect of both investors and team members. Over time, I noticed Steven's leadership style was changing—he was losing perspective on why he chose to start his company in the first place.

Steven smiled less, marveled less, and risked less. After ten years, I could hardly recognize him. As we met for coffee, Steven eventually acknowledged what I was observing. He'd become a referee. He was guarding more than guiding; he was controlling more than connecting. It is the easiest trap to fall into as a leader. The shift is slow, subtle, and sinister.

How People Respond When Led by a Referee

No doubt, every organization, just like every good football game, needs referees. In fact, the larger your organization, the more you truly need them. Someone must watch the details, establish systems and processes, and set strong boundaries. I'm speaking, however, about a mindset. Even the leaders whose jobs are to keep things in-bounds can do so (can referee) with the heart of a quarterback. When we don't, we are the ones who lose.

Research shows that young leaders want to have a career that matters. Seventy-two percent of current high school students and almost two out of three college students want to start a business. Much of the time, it's because they are socially conscious. They want to do something that matters by being the quarterback or working for a quarterback-type leader.

According to journalist Jason Haber, "Millennials have disregarded the life and career flowchart that was so formally laid out by the Baby Boomers...They don't wait to work up the corporate ladder, to start their own business. So, it should come as no surprise that they have no interest in waiting to make a difference. They inherited a flawed world and have a zeal to repair it that's unique to their generation."[1]

The point is that many young adults will turn down well-paying jobs to work for a "quarterback" that's leading a team to make a difference in the world.

I have talked to lots of young adults starting out their careers. When they don't find a quarterback leader, they often leave. Many young professionals say they are already considering a job change. People are looking for a place where they can be inspired, empowered, energized, and passionate. They're tired of working for referees who only manage by reminding them when they're out of bounds.

We all want to have that kind of leader, but are we that type of leader?

What Quarterback Leadership Looks Like

Anyone can do this because it's more about an approach than a specific job. In 2004, Scott Harrison had a crisis of conscience at age 28. Working as a club promoter in New York, he realized he was selling selfishness. So, he left his corporate job to lead in a completely different way. He became a photojournalist for a non-profit organization that provided free medical care in Africa. During his time there, he realized how many illnesses could be prevented if people just had access to clean water. In 2006, he launched charity: water to bring safe drinking water to villages that can't access it. In many ways, he has helped revolutionize how non-profit organizations raise money, and it began by empowering individuals to start their own fundraising campaigns. Scott now loves his quarterback role and enlists thousands of people to join the cause. His work is absolutely inspiring.

On the other hand, some leaders stay right where they are and change their style. Naruka Nishimatsu, the CEO of Japan Airlines observed the usual distance between him, as a leader, and the 30,000 employees working for him. Like so many, his company prioritized results more than relationships. The "flow chart" just wasn't flowing. So, what did he do? He tore down the walls of his office so anyone could walk in at any time. He now mingles with team members and customers, and he even eats meals with them. During an economic downturn, he lowered his own salary (he makes less than his pilots do). He remains accessible, travels with Japan Airlines, and always announces to the other travellers that he is the CEO, in case they have a problem. He learned how to inspire not just inspect his employees.

I recently heard about a youth soccer league that had a referee who led in a remarkable way. She came to games early enough to meet the parents and get to know them. She would even show them pictures of her own kids. She took time to meet the coaches and remind them the goal that day was to foster sportsmanship and to set an example for everyone watching. She smiled as she reminded dads that very few of these kids would go on to play professionally. In doing this, she reduced the amount of arguments from parents or coaches, inspiring them keep everything in perspective. Hmm. That referee sounds like a quarterback to me.

REFLECT AND RESPOND

1. What is it about a person that pushes them to lead like a referee as they age?

_____

_____

2. Have you ever seen a leader who migrated from a quarterback to a referee?

_____

_____

3. What have you seen leaders do to prevent themselves from leading like a referee?

_____

_____

Assess Yourself

Give yourself a candid evaluation based on the realities of your experience:

1. In what areas of your leadership would others say you're more like a referee?

    _____

    _____

2. Have you seen yourself migrate from being a quarterback to being a referee? How did it happen? What happened? When did it happen?

    _____

    _____

3. When you practice unhealthy leadership, can you put your finger on why you do so?

    _____

    _____

4. Score yourself on a scale of 1-5, with one being "never" and five being "always:"

    Do you use your position to demand loyalty?

    Never> 1   2   3   4   5 **<Always**

    Do you use your position to avoid accountability?

    Never> 1   2   3   4   5 **<Always**

    Do you use your position to manipulate behavior?

    Never> 1   2   3   4   5 **<Always**

    Do you use your position to induce guilt?

    Never> 1   2   3   4   5 **<Always**

    Do you use your position to coerce people to donate or serve?

    Never> 1   2   3   4   5 **<Always**

    Now, talk over your responses with colleagues. What changes are needed?

    _____

    _____

Try it Out: Practicing the Principle

When we stop and reflect, almost every interaction a person has with the "law" is a negative one. Not once have I seen a referee throw a flag onto the field to affirm the talent of the players. It's always about a penalty. And never have I seen a police officer pull over a driver to compliment them on the way they handle their car. Nope. It's almost always to offer a citation. This is what we expect. Unfortunately, the same reputation can surface with a person in any type of leadership role.

This week, ask at least three people who interact with you regularly to honestly evaluate their perception of your leadership. How do people view you as a leader of your club, team, class, or peers? When you approach them, do they suspect something negative has happened? Talk it over.

Then, try this habit. In every interaction you have this week, practice the following:

- INITIATE CONTACT WITH THE OTHER PERSON INSTEAD OF WAITING FOR THEM TO MAKE THE FIRST MOVE.

- FIND SOMETHING GOOD TO AFFIRM IN THE PERSON. CONNECT WITH THEM.

- OFFER A GIFT, A CONSTRUCTIVE COMMENT OR WORD OF AFFIRMATION. ADD VALUE.

- PROVIDE SOME POSITIVE DIRECTION IF THEY NEED IT. MAKE SURE YOUR COMMENTS ARE LIFE-GIVING.

After one week, reflect on your experience. How did your interactions differ from past ones?

Three Buckets

EVERYTHING THAT HAPPENS TO A LEADER FALLS INTO ONE OF THREE "BUCKETS:" WHAT IS IN THEIR CONTROL, WHAT IS OUT OF THEIR CONTROL OR WHAT IS WITHIN THEIR INFLUENCE. HEALTHY, LIFE-GIVING LEADERS EFFECTIVELY PLACE EACH EXPERIENCE IN THE CORRECT BUCKET AND ACT ACCORDINGLY: INITIATE, TRUST OR RESPOND.

When I was 19 years old, I began my career of teaching and mentoring high school students. My heart was in the right place. I didn't know much, but I sure had the right motives. I wanted to help kids. I didn't have a lot of wisdom or experience, but I had lots of passion.

I began by leading a youth group with three students: Ralph, Becky, and Keith. I served as a part-time youth worker while I worked on my bachelor's degree. When I finished four years later, the group had grown to 60 students each week. We'd made some progress.

At that point, I moved to San Diego, California, to join the staff of Dr. John C. Maxwell. While I was still teaching students, I began to recognize the importance of leadership development. I started to invest time into training student leaders and saw our department increase from an average of 60 students each week to an average of 600 young adults in two classes each week. It was fun to see that growth.

But something else happened for which I was not prepared.

I became more controlling. The evolution of my demeanor and my motives were subtle, but real. At first, I trusted my staff and volunteers entirely for everything. I had to because I was young and had nothing else to go on except trust and hope. As time marched on, however, I slowly drifted into wanting to control our program and all the results. Unwittingly, I tried to control the inputs and the outcomes. Success can be addictive. I sought to engineer every minute of our meetings, to command every line of our budget and to force progress. After all, I was the leader.

One afternoon, one of the kindest, most respectful college students in our department sat in my office and said to me, "You know, I love our department, but it seems like you're trying to control everything."

Like many others, this young woman was suffocating under my controlling leadership style.

She then asked me, "Have you observed this, too?"

I had not. In fact, I was offended.

It wasn't until later that I gained perspective about what this student had recognized. It wasn't that I was a bad person. I wasn't robbing banks or embezzling or even lying or cheating. I simply had confused my role as a leader. I wanted to control events, people, and consequences to do a good job.

Understanding the Three Buckets

What I learned from that season of my life was simple. I've come to believe that every experience we have leading others falls into one of three buckets. Each bucket represents a paradigm, requiring a very different action on the leader's part:

- It is in my control
- It is out of my control
- It is within my influence

The key to a healthy life is to place each experience in the proper bucket and to respond differently, depending on where each experience is placed.

Trouble arises when we mishandle our buckets.

Power is a strange thing. When we serve well, we tend to accrue it as a byproduct. Eventually, however, we shift our pursuit. We bypass the essential acts of service and begin yearning directly for the power. It's so easy to do. We see it on Wall Street and in Washington, D.C. We see it in youth sports leagues, non-profit organizations, corporate America, and even our homes and families.

Problems arise when we do not understand what is in our control, what is out of our control, and what is within our influence. When we assess our situations wrong, when we place them in the wrong bucket, it can lead to conflict, distrust, stalls, and turmoil. The secret to good leadership to place every situation in the right context or bucket. Items placed in the wrong bucket will prevent us from being life-giving leaders and can lead to an obsession with power and control.

"Power tends to corrupt," 19th century British historian Lord Acton said. "Absolute power corrupts absolutely."

His axiom has been vividly displayed in psychological studies over the years, most memorably the 1971 Stanford Prison Experiment. During the experiment, one group of students were arbitrarily assigned to serve as prison guards over another group of students and began to abuse their prisoners. The experiment had to be terminated once the guards took things too far. The power to control others was intoxicating.

Placing our Experiences in the Right Buckets and Responding Well

My life and leadership has been liberated since learning to place relationships and events in the proper buckets. When I do, I assume my intended role and allow others to take their proper role. Here is a summary of how leaders must respond:

Bucket One: "It is in my control. I must initiate."
Our response should be to take responsibility. If something is in my control, I must resist the temptation to avoid action or find a scapegoat to blame when things go wrong. Leaders always work in partnership with others, which means we have a role to play. We must avoid making excuses or blaming others for our mistakes. We must initiate, take proper responsibility, and own it. It's up to us to lead the way. Examples of this may be the effort you put into a task, your attitude and the words you speak.

Bucket Two: "It is out of my control. I must trust."
Our response in these circumstances is to trust. We can't force others to follow and obey us. We can't conjure up money or change the weather. We are not miracle workers. We must trust the process we are in and the people we have around us. We must not manipulate, intimidate, or dominate. In this case, we must remain committed to separate responsibility from control. Examples of this may be the conditions in which you work, other's attitudes, and perhaps even sustaining personal injuries.

Bucket Three: "It is within my influence. I must respond wisely."
Our response to this third bucket requires wisdom. It is a mixture of the first two buckets. We can't control the situation, but we can influence it. We can't force others to respond the way we want them to, to give, or to volunteer, but we can challenge them. We can't make people love us, but we can love them first and seek their response. Leadership is a dance. We lead, but they move, too. It's a volley. We can serve the ball, but they must volley back.

Many leaders, including me, enter each day carrying only our favorite bucket. We attempt to approach each person and context the same way. Some carry Bucket One because they have control issues. Others carry Bucket Two because they have trust issues. You get the idea.

Case Study: Richard Nixon and the Watergate Scandal

Do you remember hearing about the Watergate Scandal that took place in the early 1970s? President Richard Nixon was running for reelection, and a committee to put him back in office overstepped legal boundaries. While Nixon was a strong leader in many ways, this scandal is a tragic case study of a leader mishandling the three buckets.

The Break In

In May 1972, members of President Nixon's "Committee to Re-elect the President" broke into the Democratic National Committee's Watergate headquarters, stole some top-secret documents and tapped the phones. Nixon remained unaware of the details of the break-in on purpose to avoid potential ties. Sadly, he did know it was happening. But instead of insuring actions were legal and moral, he simply remained idle, ignoring the illegal activity. (**He got bucket one wrong**).

The Cover Up

Once investigative reporters started following the money in this case, they discovered what occurred and published it in their Pulitzer Prize winning book, *All the President's Men*. When questioned, Nixon's staff began to reveal who was involved, including the White House. However, Nixon delivered a speech in which he swore his staff was not involved in the break-in. Most voters believed him, and in November 1972, he was reelected in a landslide victory. Later, during Congressional hearings, it became clear the president had lied. He tried to control the consequences. It was all a cover up. (**He got bucket two wrong**).

The Reveal

When a Congressional committee asked for recordings of Nixon's conversations, he refused to release them. Later, when the Supreme Court demanded he turn them over, the truth came out. The president had known about the crime all along. Sadly, instead of using his influence well, he claimed he was "not a crook" and denied taking responsibility for his actions. In August 1974, after his role in the conspiracy was clear, Nixon finally resigned. The resolution took this long, however, because Nixon abused his position and influence to dissuade the public. This scandal changed American politics forever, leading many Americans to question their leaders and think more critically about the presidency. (**He got bucket three wrong**).

Science Confirms It...

Recent studies from UC Berkeley on the "science of power" confirm the truth of how crucial it is for leaders to manage their buckets correctly. They showed that power is wielded most effectively when used responsibly by people who are engaged with the needs of others. Years of research confirm that empathy and social intelligence are vastly more important than acquiring power through manipulation, intimidation or deception. Sadly, these studies also show that once people obtain some power, they're more likely act selfishly (*Greater Good Science Center, UCB*). The fact is, a 2012 study found that power doesn't corrupt, but it does heighten preexisting ethical tendencies. Control freaks beware: power causes us to become more of who we already are. [2]

In the end, control is not the true purpose of leadership. Life-giving leaders' influence grows when they focus on solving problems and serving people. We must draw lines in the sand and commit to never pursuing power or control. Influential leadership is always a by-product of handling our "three buckets" well as we serve others.

REFLECT AND RESPOND

1. Which of the three buckets do you see others most often mishandle?

_____

_____

2. Why do you believe leaders struggle to manage the three buckets?

_____

_____

ASSESS YOURSELF

1. In what area of your leadership would others say you are controlling?

_____

_____

2. In what area of your leadership would others say you are quick to blame others for your mistakes?

_____

_____

3. In what area of your leadership have you failed to influence wisely?

_____

_____

4. Circle your most accurate response on each line in these two columns below:

WRONG BUCKETS

1. I pursue control over people
2. I utilize manipulation and power
3. I enforce policies
4. I am cowardly in difficult times

RIGHT BUCKETS

1. I pursue connection with people
2. I leverage mission and passion
3. I empower people
4. I am courageous in difficult times

TRY IT OUT: PRACTICING THE PRINCIPLE

This week, consciously make the following shifts as you influence people:

1. Don't think **control**. Think *connect*.
2. Don't leverage **positional power**. Leverage *personal power*.
3. Don't ask, "What can I **gain**?" Instead, ask, "What can I *give*?"
4. Don't pursue **rights**. Pursue *responsibilities*.
5. Don't fight for **turf**. Fight for *trust*.
6. Don't lead by **telling**. Lead with *asking*.

After practicing these mindset shifts for a week, how did your approach to life and leadership change? Discuss these changes.

Root and Fruit

A HEALTHY TREE HAS UNSEEN ROOTS THAT STABILIZE IT AGAINST THE ELEMENTS, A TRUNK TO GIVE IT HEIGHT AND NOURISHMENT AND FRUIT TO SUBSTANTIATE ITS VALUE. LIFE-GIVING LEADERS PRIORITIZE THEIR GROWTH ELEMENTS IN THIS SAME ORDER. IT'S ABOUT "WHO" BEFORE "WHAT."

I'm no horticulturist, but I've seen some amazing plants and trees in my lifetime. For years, I lived in California, home of the famous redwood trees. I also lived in Colorado, where beautiful evergreen trees flourish in the mountains. I now reside in the South, where much of the year, you can see the lush foliage of dogwood trees, southern magnolias, and sugar maple trees. I've noticed trees have personalities just like people do. For example, there is a look, a feel, and a style you'll experience as you observe a weeping willow that is so different from that of a pine tree.

Years ago, I remember hiking in Hawaii while on vacation. My family had chosen to leave the "touristy" parts of Honolulu and see portions of the island most travelers never get to see. While near the coast, I stumbled upon a tree growing on a cliff. Because of how it was positioned at the edge of the cliff, you could not only observe its trunk and branches, but also see that the roots were exposed. I could literally examine the entire tree, below and above the ground.

This moment was an educational experience for me.

LESSONS FROM THE ROOT AND FRUIT OF TREES

The role of each part of that tree became tangibly clear and vividly important. While we rarely get to see the roots of a tree, they provide the foundation for the strength, stabilization, and life of the tree. The deeper they go, the taller it can grow. The wider they reach out beneath the ground, the more the wind can blow without taking the tree down. The strongest trees have roots that are both deep and wide. In fact, the roots govern what shape the tree will grow. The trunk and branches are all determined by what roots are growing underneath.

The trunk of the tree reflects the roots in its height and strength. Some are large in diameter. Others, not so much. But each trunk is the source of strength for branches and, ultimately, the fruit at the end of those branches. It symbolizes our performance. It's visible and eventually leads to our outcomes.

Ultimately, the branches and fruit reveal the type of tree. An apple tree or an orange tree can be identified by the small red or orange produce springing from its branches. In fact, the fruit is what substantiates that the tree is actually valuable. It's the crop. It's why you plant those trees. As musician Bob Marley wrote, "When the root is strong, the fruit is sweet."

The Who Before the What

For years, people have used the phrase, "You'll know the tree by its fruit." All trees bear fruit based on the seeds and roots in the ground. The fruit is determined by its beginnings. Show me the root, and I can tell you the fruit. Check out this diagram:

OUTCOME

PERFORMANCE

IDENTITY

This diagram is a reminder that leaders are foolish to answer the "what" question, unless they've first answered the "who" question. "What do you want to do?" is about trunks and branches, but that question is secondary. "Who are you?" is the root question and always determines everything else. The root is where it all begins.

A college student I supervised came close to a nervous breakdown. So full of angst, Cory finally caved and saw a counselor. In their meeting, he described how busy he was with a full load of classes, two part-time jobs, and a fraternity house full of expectations. No one on campus was busier than Cory. After listening to him groan about his life, the therapist diagnosed his problem. "I know what your problem is," Cory's therapist said. *"YOU'VE BECOME A 'HUMAN-DOING' BEFORE YOU'VE EVER LET YOURSELF BECOME A 'HUMAN-BEING.'"*

Wow, was she right.

Cory felt like he could fill his life with activities, answering the "what" question with a truckload of busyness and good endeavors. Sadly, it was the only question he'd asked himself. His wise counselor forced him to answer the "who" question: Who are you?

Too many leaders skip the "who" to jump right into the "what" and get busy. Oh, boy do we get busy—it is the way we are wired. After all, our teams and organizations want results, right?

Eventually, we will burn out if we don't resolve the "who" question first. It's like attaching "artificial fruit" to the branches. It may appear authentic, but its not—it is plastic and contrived (and it doesn't taste good, either).

INCARNATIONAL LEADERSHIP

During my years with John Maxwell, we discussed the diagram below several times. We referred to it as the "Incarnational Leadership" columns. Check it out:

WHO I AM? (MY BEING)	**WHAT I DO?** (MY BEHAVIOR)	**THE RESULT?** (MY OUTCOME)
1. A visionary leader	1. Set goals for the team	1. High morale on the team
2. A leader with conviction	2. Keep commitments	2. Loyal team members
3. A leader with integrity	3. Do what is right, ethical	3. Trust and momentum

The key to making the columns work efficiently is to address them from left to right—to work on our "being" and answer the "who" questions first. Our problem is that we seldom approach it this way. We are so production oriented that we leap over to the right-hand column and ask, "How do I gain high morale on my team? How do I get loyal team members? How do I earn the people's trust and gain momentum?"

We do this too often in America because we value results and productivity. We tend to focus immediately on the product instead of the process.

We'll take any fruit… even if it's artificial.

If we begin with results and outcomes and move in the wrong direction, we will be forced to conjure up all the right behaviors in that middle column, grunting and striving to set goals artificially instead of having those aspirations grow up from our identity (our natural roots). Do you know how challenging this is? Instead of goals sprouting from our identity, we fall into an ugly cycle of behavior modification, at best. We're disingenuous. It's almost impossible to sustain this over the long haul.

The solution is to start from left to right. Begin with the roots and ask, "Who am I?" Then, we behave in a way that is natural to who we are, and we'll naturally bear the fruit. The real fruit always comes from the right root. For example, look at number one. If what I am is a visionary leader, I will naturally set goals—It's what visionaries naturally tend to do. Ultimately, I will naturally experience high morale on my team. The left-hand column is the root. The middle column is the trunk. The right-hand column is the fruit.

Results are lasting when we get the order right. Healthy leaders grow from the inside out—from the roots up. Fruit is a natural outcome of a healthy identity. Effective leaders always lead this way. Stephen Covey wrote, "You can't change the fruit without changing the root." [3]

WHAT'S IN THE WAY?

Even smart people struggle with this. In the 19th century, Ralph Waldo Emerson told Henry David Thoreau, "At Harvard they teach all branches of learning." Thoreau replied, "Yes, but they don't teach the roots."

So, what are the root issues of this identity thing?

1. AWARENESS—Knowing my identity. I must be aware of my gift-mix: my personal talents, acquired skills, traits, and personality that make me unique.

2. AFFIRMATION—Hearing those I respect affirm my value. Then, I must learn to affirm myself and recognize my own value.

3. ASSOCIATION—Participating in a community where it is safe to make mistakes. Then, I must be accountable and supportive of others as I belong.

4. ACHIEVEMENT—Facing challenges and using my strengths. I must find ways to add value to others through those gifts.

Leadership professor Warren Bennis said it best. "Becoming a leader is synonymous with becoming yourself. It is precisely that simple and it is also that difficult," Bennis said. [4]

The truth is, most of us don't stop to ask the "who" question, or if we do, we don't like the answer. It isn't flashy enough, so we pretend to be like someone else and don't become the best version of ourselves. Actor Sean Connery was once asked why he kept acting, even though he's got plenty of money. His response? "Because I get the opportunity to be somebody better and more interesting than I am."

I wonder how many of us are acting and might confess to the same thing?

Reflect and Respond

1. Why is it challenging for us to focus on the root (our identity) first?

_____

_____

2. What coerces leaders to jump right into the "what" question and become busy?

_____

_____

3. Have you seen a leader get this process right and lead out of a healthy identity?

_____

_____

Assess Yourself

As you reflect on your own identity, indicate which areas below you've wrestled with as a person and leader. A healthy sense of identity includes four elements:

Identity Element:	If Missing, I Feel:	Do You Struggle?
1. A sense of worth	1. Inferior	_____
2. A sense of belonging	2. Insecure	_____
3. A sense of competence	3. Inadequate	_____
4. A sense of purpose	4. Insignificant	_____

Which of these four elements do you struggle with the most?

_____

_____

TRY IT OUT: PRACTICING THE PRINCIPLE

This week, find ways to practice the four elements of healthy identity roots:

1. AWARENESS—Knowing who I am and my personal strengths.

   How can you practice this?

2. AFFIRMATION—Hearing others affirm my value and affirming my own value.

   How can you practice this?

3. ASSOCIATION—Participating in a community that is safe and stretching for me.

   How can you practice this?

4. ACHIEVEMENT—Facing challenges and adding value with my strengths and gifts.

   How can you practice this?

Which ones did you have the most trouble practicing? Share your findings with a mentor or peer and discuss a plan for growth.

IMAGE FOUR
[Surgeons and Vampires]

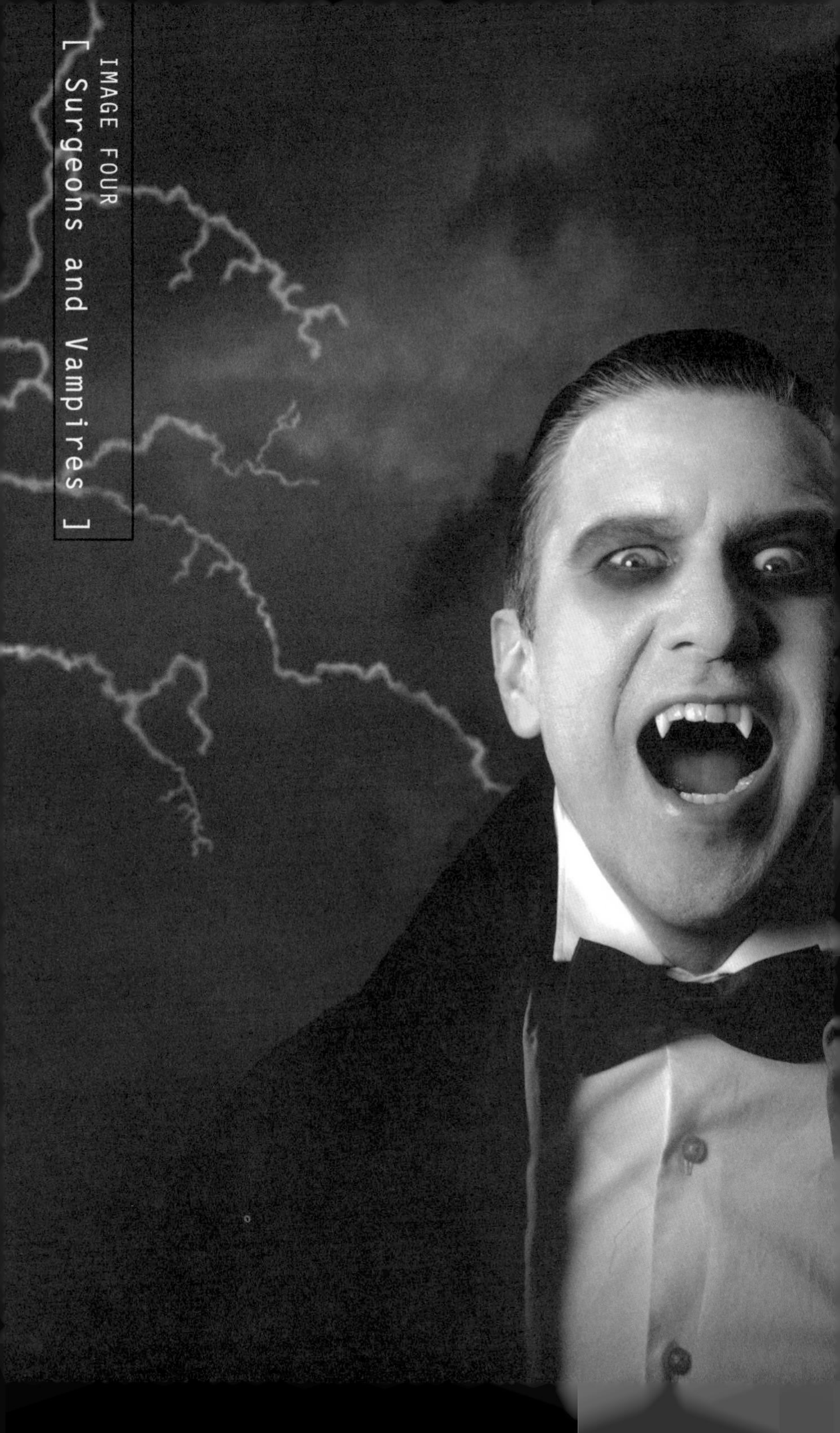

IMAGE FOUR

[Surgeons or Vampires]

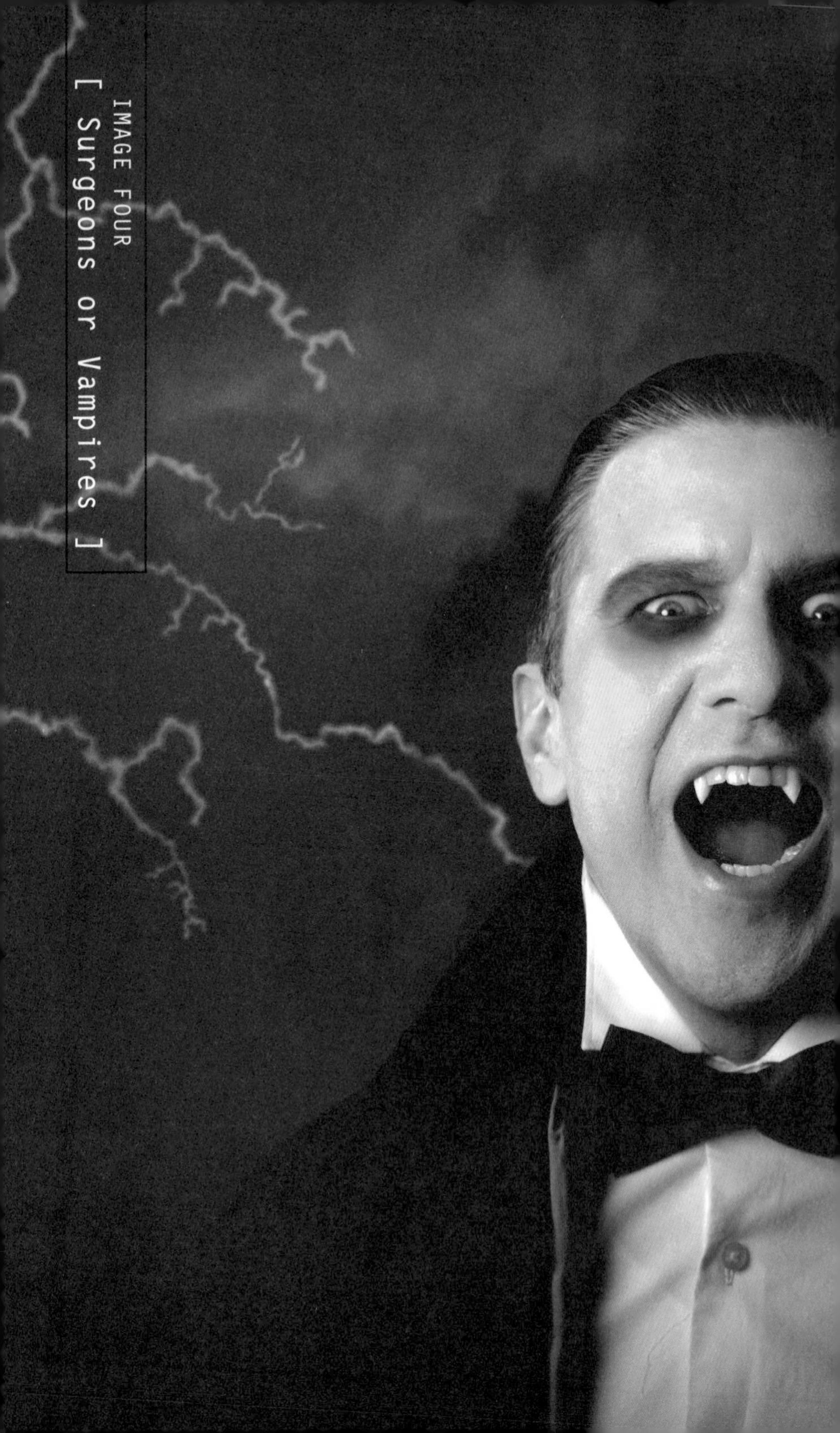

Surgeons and Vampires

THERE IS A RIGHT AND WRONG WAY TO OFFER FEEDBACK OR CRITICISM TO
PEOPLE. VAMPIRES SUCK THE LIFEBLOOD RIGHT OUT OF A PERSON, OPERATING
FROM THEIR OWN NEED. SURGEONS TAKE BLOOD TO TREAT MEDICAL CONDITIONS
CAREFULLY AND CONSTRUCTIVELY. THOUGH BOTH DRAW BLOOD, THEY LEAD TO
COMPLETELY DIFFERENT OUTCOMES.

I'm sure you've noticed the major comeback vampires have made in the media
over the last twenty years. TV shows and movies have included several of those
mythical parasites preying on their unsuspecting victims. For some reason, people
seem to be entertained by it all. Vampires have been popular since the silent film
era, long before Buffy was around to slay them.

At the same time, shows about doctors or surgeons have also been popular. I
can't remember a time when there wasn't a drama about hospitals and medical
professionals on TV. I wonder if our culture's fascination with both vampires and
physicians illustrates that people are strangely drawn to stories that involve blood?
And that curious fascination is a good starting point for this *Habitude*.

Blood has always symbolized life. We even see this idea in the term "lifeblood."
Physiologically, we know that blood circulates through our bodies, enabling us to
function, to breathe, to live.

This allows for an instructive comparison and contrast between vampires and
surgeons. Have you ever taken a moment to consider that both draw blood when
they perform? Both can be sources of pain, both break the skin, and both usually
elicit stress for anyone who encounters them. Why? Because, no matter which one
you run into, you are going to lose some blood. Beyond the blood loss, however,
there is a huge difference between the surgeon and vampire.

OFFERING FEEDBACK TO OTHERS

The work of a vampire has a consequence. The work of a doctor leads to a benefit.
Traditionally, vampires prey on unsuspecting victims, biting them on the neck
with their fangs. In folklore, vampires are defined by their need to feed on blood
and are driven by their manipulative nature. This theme has remained common
throughout the many film adaptations over the last century. A surgeon, on the

other hand, carefully selects where the incision will go. The operation is done prudently and meticulously, cautiously treating a specific condition and sewing the skin back together so healing can result. With surgeons, the pain leads to gain.

My friend Brett Trapp first brought this idea to my attention. Poor leaders offer feedback a little bit like a vampire. Life-giving leaders do so like a surgeon, even when the feedback is critical and corrective. They draw blood so that life and health can be restored to their team members. One takes life. The other gives life.

How do you offer feedback to your team? Like a vampire or a surgeon?

Leading in High Stress Situations

We live in a day of elevated stress levels. Whether it's a school campus, a sports team, or a workplace, the stakes feel high, and just being on a team can often raise our anxiety. Because the competition is fierce, teams are constantly under pressure to improve or get left in the dust. This can lead to impatience, frustration, poor communication, and angst.

According to Robert Leahy, Director of the American Institute of Cognitive Therapy, the average teen today has the same anxiety level as the average psychiatric patient did in the 1950s. The level of stress we feel can foster "vampire style" leadership. Not only that, I often meet adults who are irritated at students and dissatisfied with their output. They claim young leaders don't display resilience; they act entitled, don't follow through on commitments, and are frequently just plain lazy. Of course, any of these realities are likely to create "high-stress interactions," but in the midst of these very interactions, we have two choices of how to respond.

There are two common scenarios that surface in stressful contexts:

1. Most tend to lead out of **relief**.
2. The successful tend to lead out of ***belief***.

The Motivation of Relief

Leading out of relief is what a "vampire" leader does. The goal is to satisfy an appetite or relieve stress. Parents do this when their kids exhaust them. Employers do this when they vent at young staffers who don't perform. You might be tempted to do this when you are feeling the pressure of school, work, or everyday life. You may simply feel overwhelmed. In these moments, we often want to relieve the current negative emotions we feel.

Sadly, while relief is the quicker and easier option, it is not the long-term solution. Just like a vampire, this type of leadership aims to quickly satisfy a pressing appetite.

WE TEND TO BE MOTIVATED BY RELIEVING THE PAIN RATHER THAN BELIEVING IN THE PERSON. IT'S USUALLY ONE OR THE OTHER—RELIEF OR BELIEF.

Relief is our natural default style of leadership. When facing a difficult situation, we seek to ease the pain, to get a quick fix for ourselves and for those that we lead. Our goal is to relieve the tension. The point is that without intention, we can all be natural vampires.

At times, it's about our relief. We choose the easy route and appease others, giving in to their requests. It makes life easier, at least in the moment. And sometimes, we lead out of relief by venting our anger. Sadly, anger is punitive rather than redemptive.

And sometimes, it's about their relief. We want to relieve others of the consequences that come with poor choices or behaviors because they're so stressed out. As you know, students have so many pressures on them with grades, sports, and standardized tests. When you empathize with others' situations, it feels right to let them off the hook. And while it does ease their pain temporarily, it doesn't empower those under your leadership to grow and improve. Sadly, this approach is permissive rather than redemptive.

In short, venting feels good to me and lets me off hook. Caving feels good to them and lets them off the hook. Both reactions compromise good leadership. I'm like a vampire.

THE MOTIVATION OF BELIEF

In a challenging situation, "surgeon" leaders operate out of fundamental belief in the potential of those they lead. We pull out the best in them when we believe the best about them. Research from psychologist, Diana Baumrind, from U.C. Berkeley reminds us that people are most productive when we are both responsive and demanding.

1. RESPONSIVE TO THEM—We are attentive, supportive, and caring. We love, understand, and believe in them.

2. DEMANDING OF THEM—Because we believe in them, we cannot allow them settle for less than their best. We hold them to high standards. [5]

This is what every human being needs. As you seek to become a life-giving leader, one of the most important skills to master is knowing when to be responsive to the needs of those you lead and when to demand the best out of them.

Often, we must do both at the same time.

Daniel Coyle and a team of psychologists from Stanford, Yale and Columbia explored the concept of feedback and which type received the best results. They asked middle school teachers to give a writing project to their students and afterward, offer them various types of responses. To their surprise, the researchers discovered there was one particular approach to criticism that improved effort so much they labeled it "magical." Students who received this feedback chose to revise their papers far more often than students who did not—a 40 percent increase among white students and a 320 percent boost among minority students. In the end, it improved performances significantly. [6] The approach to criticism was rather simple. Teachers explained that they had high expectations of their students: *I'M GIVING YOU THESE COMMENTS BECAUSE I HAVE HIGH EXPECTATIONS OF YOU AND I KNOW YOU CAN REACH THEM.*

Of course, the words are not magic, but the thought behind them is profound. They communicated the challenge from a fundamental belief in their students. You and I can adopt this type of life-giving leadership as well, but it will require tough love with patience and tenacity to follow through. It's effective when our leadership stems from a deep-seated belief in those we are leading.

I once heard a story about an important figure in American history that—whether it is urban legend or fact—continues to inspire me as a teacher and leader. Thomas Edison is said to have shared the circumstances of how he became such an incredible inventor. When young Tom returned home from school one day, his mother noticed he had a piece of paper in his hand. It was a note from his teacher, and his mom was the only one who was supposed to read it. When she did, she grew tearful. Predictably, the boy asked what it said.

His mother paused, then replied, "Your son is a genius. This school is too small for him and doesn't have enough good teachers to train him. Please teach him yourself."

From then on, Edison's mom removed him from school, and he was self-taught. She allowed him to curiously pursue what interested him and to devour it.

Years later, after his mom died, Edison was rummaging through her belongings and came across that note from his teacher. When he read it, he was stunned. It read, "Your son is addled (mentally ill). We won't let him come to school anymore. We don't have the teachers to handle him. You'll have to teach him yourself."

Edison wept for hours and since that time, gave his mother credit for cultivating his genius as an inventor. She saw something in her son that others didn't. What she read to him and what that note actually said ultimately led to the same result: Tom had to learn at home. But, the belief behind that circumstance meant everything to him.

Someone had chosen to believe in him.

1. Why is it leaders get anxious and often lead like vampires instead of surgeons?

_____

_____

2. What prevents us from seeing the potential in someone and believing in them?

_____

_____

ASSESS YOURSELF

After reviewing the two columns, mark an X on the line that accurately describes you:

WHEN I AM A VAMPIRE	WHEN I AM A SURGEON
1. I am thinking about me	1. I am thinking about you
2. I may use sarcasm or hyperbole	2. I will be careful and accurate
3. I surprise the person as I attack	3. I carefully plan our encounter
4. I look backward at a past flaw	4. I look forward to future possibilities
5. I may assault the person's character	5. I cautiously remove the problem
6. Short-term gain; long-term pain	6. Short term-pain; long-term gain

In times of crisis, would those around you describe you as more of a surgeon or vampire? Be honest as you place an X on the spectrum below.

VAMPIRE -- SURGEON

TRY IT OUT: PRACTICING THE PRINCIPLE

When we lead out of "belief" we produce superior results. Next week, attempt to prepare for every discussion you have with those you are leading by asking yourself the following questions:

- WHAT MUST BE SAID OR DONE TO DISPLAY MY BELIEF IN THEM?
- HOW WOULD I HANDLE A LESS-THAN-OPTIMAL PERFORMANCE IF I GENUINELY BELIEVED THEY COULD PERFORM BETTER?
- HOW WOULD MY WORDS CHANGE?

Keep a log of how your conversations and results change over seven days. Talk about it with other leaders. What happened?

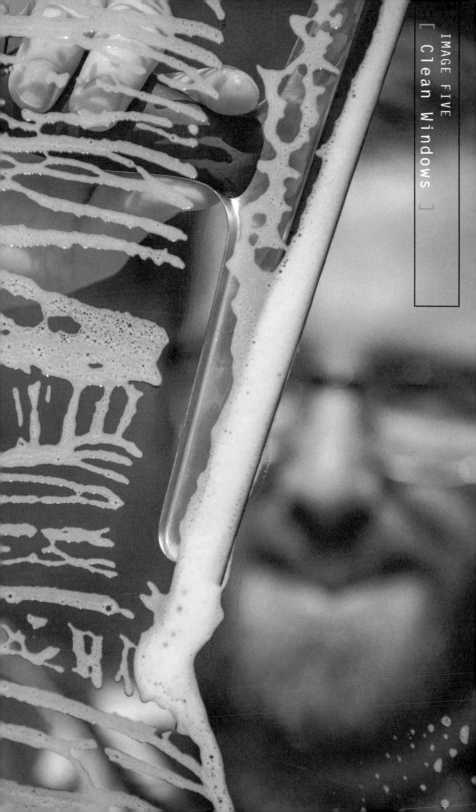

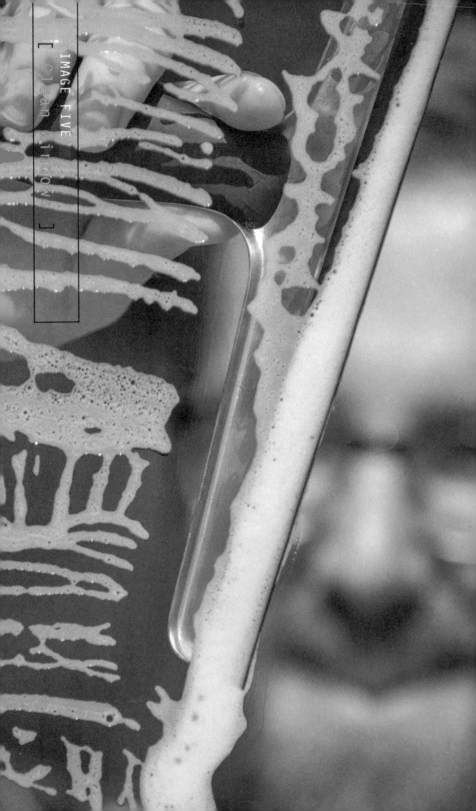

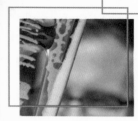

Clean Windows

IS THE WORD "CLEAN" A VERB OR AN ADJECTIVE? IS IT AN ACTION OR A GOAL? DO YOU WANT YOUR TEAM TO "CLEAN THE WINDOWS" OR DO YOU WANT "CLEAN WINDOWS" AS AN END GOAL? EFFECTIVE LEADERS COMMUNICATE CLEAR OUTCOMES. THEY ARE DESCRIPTIVE RATHER THAN PRESCRIPTIVE IN THEIR VISION.

Every leader has struggled with good people who misinterpret their direction or vision. Often, leaders give instructions only to have team members disappoint them in their execution of those orders. Consider this scenario: When you ask someone to "wipe down the windows," they will wipe them down. The window may end up with streaks all over it or smudges in certain places, but the person gave you exactly what you asked for—they wiped the windows down. If instead, you ask a team member to "make the window crystal clear," they will deliver what you asked for—a beautiful "crystal clear" window.

However, if the objective is clear enough, how they clean that window should be up to them.

MANAGEMENT BY OBJECTIVE

The key to having "clean windows" is to manage by objective. Instead of telling people what to do, lasting leaders describe the outcome they hope for and allow the person to surprise them with their innovation. This requires our leadership to be "descriptive" not "prescriptive." We must stop prescribing every step along the way, as if we were doing the task. Instead, we should describe the result we want and let those great team members demonstrate what they can do. This allows them to put on display the gifts, creativity, and energy they possess by owning how they reach the goal.

There are, of course, some inexperienced team members that will need leaders to be prescriptive in their instruction. In those cases, leaders must suggest particular steps they should take. Most of the time, however, we leaders tend to micromanage and require team members to pursue goals in the exact same manner we would ourselves. The result is that team members often don't "own" the goal. They are simply trudging through a task we own that they are merely renting from us.

"Management by objective" occurs when a leader describes an outcome they want to see happen—an objective they desire accomplished—and they turn a team member loose to go after it in their own way. The benefits of this style of leadership are many:

- THE TEAM MEMBERS GET TO USE THEIR CREATIVITY AND GIFTS.
- THE TEAM MEMBERS BEGIN TO "OWN" THE PROJECT.
- THE TEAM MEMBERS LIKELY ACHIEVE THE GOAL FASTER DOING IT THEIR WAY.
- THE TEAM MEMBERS INVEST MORE ENERGY BECAUSE THEY CHOSE THE METHOD.

From the beginning of our organization—Growing Leaders—I knew my best style of leadership for both interns and our young team members was "management by objective." In fact, I prefer hiring college upperclassmen or recent graduates instead of freshmen as interns simply because they're often more mature and ready for the ownership necessary under this kind of leadership style.

SITUATIONAL LEADERSHIP

Years, ago, authors Ken Blanchard and Paul Hersey coined the term "situational leadership." It's a model explaining that people respond better to various kinds of leadership, based on their experience and maturity. While the theory was developed in the 1970s, it has evolved over time. [7] Here are the four styles:

Style 1—Telling
This is a more directive style, characterized by one-way instruction, defining the role of the person and providing the what, how, when, and where of the task at hand.

Style 2—Selling
This is a more interactive style, using two-way conversation to define the task and providing support that allows the person to buy into the project.

Style 3—Participating
This is a more relational style, issuing fewer task behaviors and engaging both the leader and the person to determine how the job will be done.

Style 4—Delegating
This style is empowering, as it relays the outcome you desire but leaves the methods and responsibility to the individual. The leader is only a monitor.

Over time, leaders should consistently cast the vision, define the culture, and embody the values so they can move toward Style 3 and Style 4 with their team members. When team members constantly see excellence modeled by leaders and hear it communicated as a goal, they're more apt to display it themselves. We must help them to see what we see, love what we love, and desire what we desire.

Antoine de Saint-Exupery once said, "If you want to build a ship, don't herd people together to collect wood and don't assign them tasks and work, but rather, teach them to long for the endless immensity of the sea."

What This Looks Like in Real Life

Years ago, an executive at the Six Flags Over Georgia theme park heard that his custodial staff was providing horrible customer service at their amusement park. Guests were complaining about their attitudes and tempers. So, the executive did something interesting: he dressed up like a custodian and joined the staff for a day.

No one recognized him, and he could discover what was going on, incognito. After just one day on the job, the executive understood the problem. The custodians had merely been following the steps they'd been given. They believed their job was to keep the park clean. Since the patrons always messed it up, they quickly became the enemy. Custodians, in turn, became adversarial toward those customers. The result, of course, was that everyone was resentful.

Once back in his office, the executive did some re-training with the staff. He taught them that the ultimate goal was to please the customers. Period. Now, obviously, those customers enjoy a clean park, but that was secondary. Soon, their service improved measurably. They saw the big picture and began to "own" the executive's vision.

You might say, that executive shifted from saying "clean the windows" to saying, "Do whatever you must to make sure the windows are crystal clear at all times."

For leaders, the shift must be to:

- Focus on "outcomes" (ultimate goals) rather than "inputs" (specific tasks).
- Focus on scoring accomplishments, not merely doing activities.
- Focus on teaching them how to think, not just what to think.
- Focus on describing a goal, not prescribing a behavioral role.

"Make sure all the windows in the front of our store are crystal clear at all times," is a much better goal than telling employees to "wipe down the windows when you get a chance." The second statement is plain and simple but does not expect much from the recipient. They are merely following orders. They might even do the bare minimum. The first directive above expects excellence and clearly states the desired outcome, while also leaving the execution of the task up to the person to whom it is assigned. They become "owners" of both the vision and the task.

It is unwise to expect someone to be the owner and leader when you have only asked for them to be a follower.

Years ago, I accidentally discovered this reality.

I was mentoring a community of university students when one of them sent me an email asking who was choosing the topic for the next week's session. I was teaching leadership strategies to this group, and up until then, I had facilitated each lesson as their instructor. After all, that's my job. When I saw the inquiry, I grabbed my laptop and typed in my response: "I can do that."

Or, at least that's what I meant to say.

Without knowing it, however, I had mistyped: the letter "i" on my keyboard is right next to the letter "u." Unwittingly, I sent the message back: "u can do that."

And he believed me.

At our next meeting, the students showed up ready to go. Before I could interrupt them, they proceeded to facilitate the discussion, the experiments, the learning and the outcomes. They were brilliant. In fact, they didn't even need me. I had never felt such satisfaction than in that meeting when my "mentees" taught themselves. They felt empowered because I sent the message, "u can do that."

I never told them it was an accident on my part.

When we set expectations (high or low), people usually perform to them. It all begins with the vision we cast and the way we ask them to engage. In the end, "clean windows" should always be a description (of their work's outcome) not a direction (of the task they're supposed to do). It should be an outcome, not an input. It's a very average piece of instruction but an excellent point of description of a job well done. Activity does not equal accomplishment.

Two out of three people are visual learners, so when given a vision of a preferred future, they will perform better than when given mere steps to follow. A vision allows their imagination to take over, spurring them on to results they never thought possible. It just takes a leader with the courage to cast a vision and turn them loose.

Now, let's go find out how clean those windows can actually be.

Reflect and Respond

1. Why do so many leaders lead with specific steps rather than with vision? Why is there a tendency to just say, "Clean the windows?"

_____

_____

2. Why do so many team members fail to catch a vision for excellence from their leader?

_____

_____

3. How have you been led in the past? When you were new on the job, did you have supervisors who merely said, "Clean the windows," or did you have one who offered you a vision?

_____

_____

Assess Yourself

Reflect on your leadership. Mark an X at the point on the line that accurately describes you:

1. I find myself naturally leading others by describing detailed steps for completing tasks.

   FALSE -- TRUE

2. I tend to micromanage team members because they often don't see the big picture.

   FALSE -- TRUE

3. I'm not good at trusting others with a task that I delegate.

   FALSE -- TRUE

4. I find it difficult to cast a vision for an excellent outcome.

   FALSE -- TRUE

Try it Out: Practicing the Principle

This week, I'd like to suggest a game plan for your leadership: List a handful of important projects that someone on your team could accomplish if you delegated that project well. Next, write out a clear description of how the task would look if done with excellence—jot down your vision for the project if you were putting your best effort into it. Then, take that "vision" as an outcome (clean windows), meet with an appropriately gifted team member, and use that as a guide in your delegation. If they need suggestions on steps to take, go ahead and offer them, but only if they ask. When these projects are finished, evaluate what happened.

IMAGE SIX

[Salutes and Snubs]

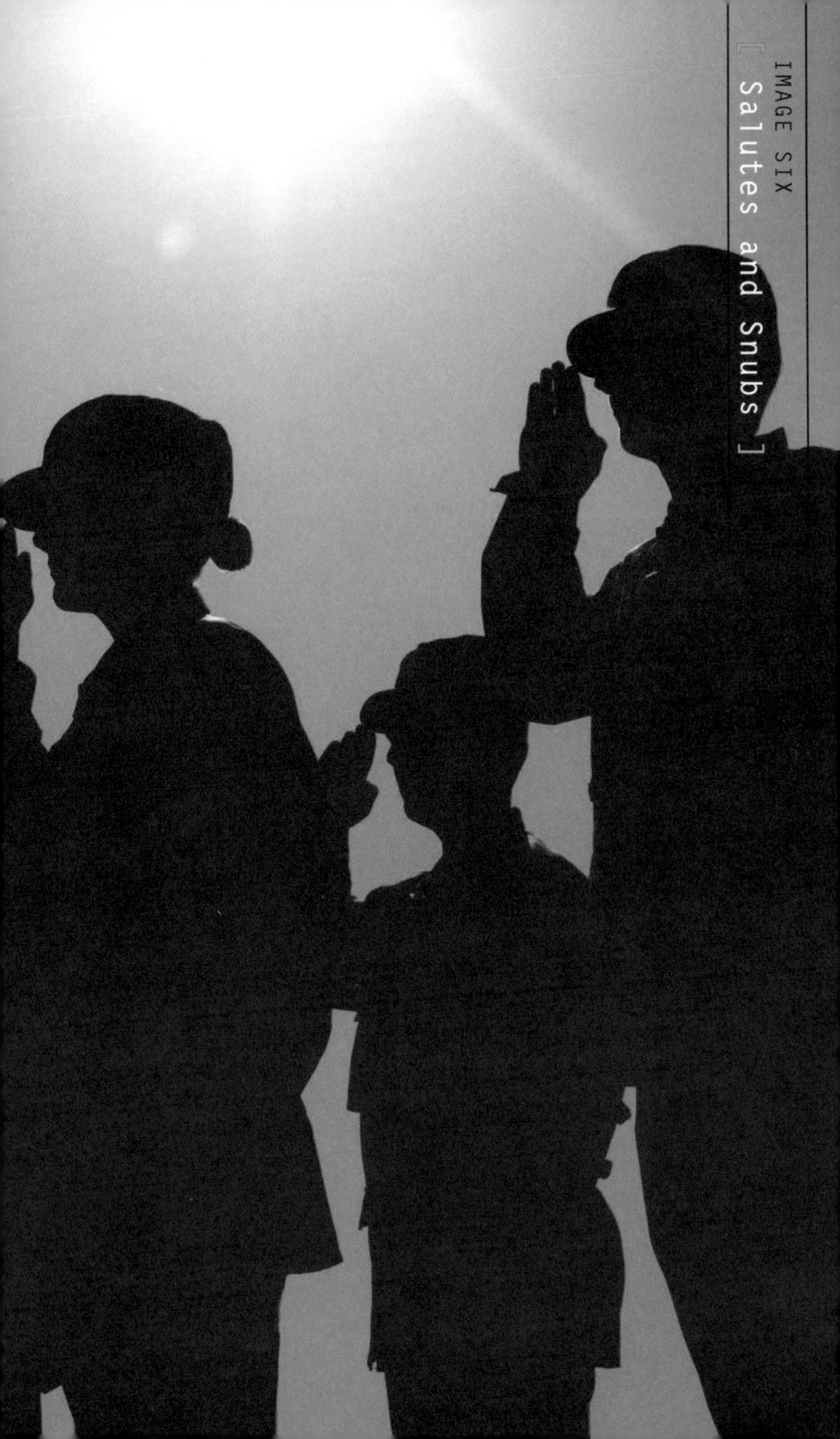

[Salutes and Snubs]

Salutes and Snubs

IN THE MILITARY, THE HIGHEST FORM OF GREETING IS A SALUTE AND IS USUALLY RESERVED FOR OFFICERS. LIFE-GIVING LEADERS REMOVE THE RANKS OF TEAM MEMBERS AND TREAT EVERYONE, REGARDLESS OF STATUS, WITH COMPLETE RESPECT—SALUTING OTHERS AS OFFICERS INSTEAD OF SNUBBING THEM AS ROOKIES.

We've all seen military soldiers salute someone of a higher rank as they enter the room. In military traditions throughout history, there have been numerous methods of performing salutes: hand gestures, hoisting flags, or maybe removing headgear. The nature of the salute is the acknowledgement that someone deserving deference and honor has walked into your presence.

I will never forget, as a young boy, watching the funeral service for President John F. Kennedy on television. Soldiers from all branches of our military stopped to salute the casket of their former commander in chief before saluting the other officers present. It was an incredible display of respect and reverence. They conducted themselves as if they were in the presence of nobility.

There are two memorable accounts of the origin of our modern salute.

Some historians believe it dates back to European monarchies. When citizens saw their queen approaching, they would raise their hand just above their eyes, as if to shield their eyes from the bright glow of her face. Obviously, there was no real glow, but it was a gesture of honor. It was a visual response to the queen's "radiant beauty," which required those nearby to create shade above their eyes, just as we might do when looking into a sunny sky.

According to current military manuals, the modern Western salute originated when knights greeted each other. To signal friendly intentions, they would raise their visors to show their faces—a salute of sorts. Others also note that raising your visor was a way to identify yourself by saying, "This is who I am, and I'm not afraid."

In both cases, the salute was a sign of relationship and respect.

The person saluting was saying, "I acknowledge and honor you, and I am revealing my good intentions."

Today's Vanishing Salute

In our world today, displays of respect are diminishing. Our culture is far less formal than in the past. We wear casual clothes at work or while traveling more than we did a century ago, we use more familiar language—even with strangers—and we greet people with a more personal tone than salutations from the 19th and 20th centuries. In one sense, this can be seen as a step in the right direction. No one likes people who act stuffy. The Victorian Age is, indeed, a thing of the past.

Sadly, however, these casual displays do have a downside.

In most places, the natural respect we once demonstrated for the elderly or for authorities is in decline. In public transportation, we need signs to remind us to allow older or disabled people to have our seat on the train. We don't naturally practice respectful manners unless we've been taught to do so. When we talk to people, we seldom maintain good eye contact. In fact, we now hide behind technology to snub others. It happens all the time.

Focusing on your phone in a social setting is known as "phubbing"—which is a combination of "phone" and "snubbing." A relatively new study published in the journal *Computers in Human Behavior* examined what motivates people to "phub" and how it seems to have become a normal part of life. It's a lazy person's way of avoiding social contact. People will commonly just stare at their phone instead of acknowledging someone right next to them. [8]

Most of us have probably snubbed someone in our past. It is the opposite of respect. It means to pay no attention and to ignore the presence of someone, offering no acknowledgment, but treating them with contempt or neglect.

It is no coincidence that the words "snub" and "snob" are pronounced so similarly. If you've been on the other side of snubbing, you know it doesn't feel very good.

Snubbing is often the new normal. Friendships or dating relationships frequently end when someone simply stops texting or messaging the other. When we don't know how to have a hard conversation, we merely choose to have no conversation. We avoid. We ignore. We snub. It's socially easier than showing respect.

Great teams fight "snubbing" and find ways to "salute" each other.

Respect is a Choice

When I talk to college students, they usually explain their lack of respect toward professors, police, or politicians by saying those individuals have not earned their respect. They've acted in a way that doesn't deserve our esteem. Very often, I agree. However, I have come to believe that respect must be a choice. It's something we choose to give, not something we demand others to earn all the time. While I believe leaders should act in a respectful manner, our culture makes progress only when we determine to give respect as a rule, not an exception.

Respect should be given unconditionally.

When we do that, I believe respect breeds respect.

I vividly remember the 1968 presidential election between Richard Nixon and Hubert Humphrey. The Republican and Democrat candidates saw issues very differently but cultivated a friendship during their political careers. Despite their differences, they called and visited each other over the years—asking about each other's families, laughing at jokes, and talking about vacations. In 1972, when President Nixon was reelected, one of the first calls he got was from Humphrey congratulating him on his victory. What I remember most, however, was when Hubert Humphrey died in 1978. Photos from the funeral appeared on the news, and Richard Nixon—his political opponent—sat next to his Humphrey's wife, Muriel, during the memorial. Once again, it's a great picture of two leaders finding a way to salute each other.

THE PECKING ORDER

If you were to ask someone, "Who deserves respect?" they might commonly say it depends on one or all of three categories:

1. RESULTS—We feel if someone's talent produces results, they deserve respect.

2. RELATIONSHIP—We feel if someone is closely connected to us, they deserve respect.

3. RANK—We feel if someone has a higher spot in the flow chart, they deserve respect.

The "pecking order" is a widespread and common approach to respect. It is logical to most people, even if they fail to practice it. Unfortunately, this view often leads us to excuse ourselves from showing respect to those who don't qualify for it.

But, what if you lived differently? What if you did away with perceived rank and treated everyone like a VIP? What if everyone received the respect of an officer? What if the star player on the team and the last guy on the bench were both respected by the entire team? What if the celebration for winning included everyone equally?

Our research reveals these six results when that happens:

- MORALE GOES UP TANGIBLY
- ETHICS AND WORK ETHIC RISES
- CAMARADERIE INCREASES
- SACRIFICE ON BEHALF OF THE TEAM RISES
- COLLABORATION SKYROCKETS
- PRODUCTION EXPANDS AMONG THE TEAM

I believe I owe everyone a basic level of respect for being fellow human beings but realize that my level of respect will vary from person to person. We all know, by nature, that we tend to hold some people in higher regard for who they are and what they've done. But actually, our level of respect has less to do with who they are and more to do with who we are.

In short, respect begins with self-respect.

If I don't possess a level of self-respect, if I can't look in the mirror and genuinely admire the face staring back at me, my respect for others will diminish. At best, our show of respect will be artificial. I cannot give away what I don't have. We must respect ourselves before we can enjoy what I've described in this chapter. Laurence Stone summarized the role of each this way:

> *"RESPECT FOR OURSELVES GUIDES OUR MORALS;*
> *RESPECT FOR OTHERS GUIDES OUR MANNERS."* [9]

You likely remember NFL quarterback Colin Kaepernick who sat down on the bench instead of standing during the national anthem during the 2016—2017 football season. This led to a firestorm from angry fans who felt he was disrespecting the flag and the military. Colin was simply protesting social injustice and police brutality. This episode has bred further controversy, but it's the story behind Kaepernick's story that I appreciate most.

A former Army Green Beret named Nate Boyer wrote an open letter to Colin explaining how his actions felt disrespectful. Colin replied by saying he never meant to disrespect anyone, but he believed the freedom and equality the military fought for wasn't being honored for all Americans. This led to a great meeting where Colin and Nate listened to each other and spoke their minds. The result? Nate suggested Colin could still protest by taking a knee rather than sitting on the bench. Taking a knee is a common act a soldier might observe for a fallen brother, like flying a flag at half-staff. It means that a brother has died. This solution allowed both sides to feel they were respected, but it required two men with opposing views to salute each other.

REFLECT AND RESPOND

1. Do you think people tend to show less respect for others today than we did in the past? Why or why not?

_____

_____

2. How do you think people decide on who deserves respect?

_____

_____

3. What happens when team members snub each other and fail to show respect?

_____

_____

4. What are specific ways your team members could "salute" each other and show respect for one another?

_____

_____

5. What would your team look like if everyone both gave and received respect from each other?

_____

_____

Assess Yourself

Take a minute and think about how you give and receive respect. On a scale of one to ten (ten being the strongest), rate yourself in the following areas:

1. Self Respect (I practice discipline in my physical, mental, and emotional health.)

   1   2   3   4   5   6   7   8   9   10

2. Respect for Authority (I consistently display honor to all in a role of authority.)

   1   2   3   4   5   6   7   8   9   10

3. Respect for Team (I demonstrate respect for all team members, no matter what.)

   1   2   3   4   5   6   7   8   9   10

4. Respect for Everyone (In general, I show respect to others as fellow humans.)

   1   2   3   4   5   6   7   8   9   10

Why did you give yourself the scores you did?

Do some creative thinking. Identify one clear way you can communicate respect for yourself, your teammates or coworkers, your coaches or supervisors, and your fellow human beings.

Each display of respect may be unique, but practice them daily for one week. Ask someone to hold you accountable to follow through. Next, as a team, brainstorm some ways that everyone can "salute" each other and show respect. Afterwards, discuss the results. Did it raise morale? Did it feel fake? How could you make it a genuine habit for several weeks? How did your self-respect change by "saluting" others in your circle of influence? Talk about a customized salute for your team.

Splashes and Waves

MANY LEADERS STEP ON THE PLATFORM AND SIMPLY MAKE A SPLASH, BUT ANYONE CAN DO THAT—NOTHING CHANGES. LIFE-GIVING LEADERS MAKE WAVES. THEIR WORK AND WORDS IGNITE MOVEMENTS THAT MOBILIZE TEAM MEMBERS TO BECOME THE BEST VERSIONS OF THEMSELVES.

I lived in San Diego, California, as a teen and through most of my early career. As you likely know, San Diego is a beautiful city with near perfect weather and is located next to the Pacific Ocean. Every summer the beaches and bays are full of swimmers, surfers, and sailors enjoying America's gigantic West Coast pool.

I recall the first time I visited the beach at ten years old. I was so excited to be at a Southern California beach that I ran into the water and began splashing everywhere and everyone. Excitement levels were high, and my self-awareness was low. I was completely unaware of how my splashes affected anyone around me. I was amused, while others became annoyed.

Suddenly, I noticed everyone looking out to the sea, their eyes growing bigger. When I finally turned to look for myself, it was too late. A mammoth wave came crashing in, knocking me over (along with anyone else who wasn't paying attention). I quickly learned that those ocean waves are powerful.

Obviously, I was powerless against that big wave. No matter how hard I tried that afternoon, I could not remain standing when a wave hit. The wave conquered me. I was a victim of its strength. I quickly discovered that all my splashing was nothing compared to the might of an incoming wave.

This illustration is also a picture of leadership. You see, there are two kinds of leaders: those who make splashes and those who make waves.

THE SPLASHERS

You've probably seen them both up front on a stage. The splashers are the ones who know some gimmicks and have some guts. They've got tricks up their sleeve, and their goal is to impress a crowd and entertain. They yearn for their audience to like them. They are so intent on this goal that they often go to extreme lengths to reach it—off the wall and on the edge techniques crafted to get the listeners to talk about them, tweet about them, blog about them, and take selfies with them. They won't admit it, but their secret ambition is to become mini-celebrities.

THE WAVE-MAKERS

Leaders who make waves actually foster genuine life change. It isn't just about the momentary laughter at a conference or meeting; it's about moving people from one place to another. They catalyze permanent transformation by creating environments that equip people to actually live life differently. They're humble, authentic, life-giving leaders who want to call attention to others rather than themselves. They also understand that while "splashes" happen in a moment and cause excitement, waves build over time, starting small and becoming large in the end.

In short, leaders who make splashes are about momentary events and leaders who cause waves are about building a recurring process. A great event can happen overnight. A great process happens over time.

EVENTS AND PROCESS

Check out the two columns below. They summarize the role of both splashes and waves. We need both great events and great processes to follow those events to spark progress. An event can take place in a single day, but a process where true life change occurs happens over a period of weeks and months. Maybe years. Events are glitzy. Process is unglamorous. We need both, but far too often, we're good at hosting events but poor at creating a process.

THE EVENT	THE PROCESS
1. Motivates people	1. Matures people
2. Encourages decisions	2. Encourages development
3. Is a calendar issue	3. Is a consistency issue
4. Challenges people	4. Changes people
5. Usually about a big group	5. Usually about a small group
6. Is about information	6. Is about interaction
7. Becomes a catalyst	7. Becomes a culture
8. Easy to pull off	8. Difficult to pull off

You can see from the columns above that both are necessary, but many leaders have become far too preoccupied with only putting on sizzling events. Events slowly fade in our memories and really don't change us. They sizzle and then they fizzle. This happens at big conferences, assemblies, retreats, rallies, summer camps, and concerts.

A Sad Confession

You would have enjoyed listening to Ted (not his real name). He was a dynamic speaker who motivated business professionals for most of his career. Three years ago, I attended Ted's funeral. It was a bittersweet experience for me because I was among many people who loved his unforgettable style, his gimmicks for amusing a crowd, and his infectious laugh. But Ted acknowledged something to me, just before he passed away. He told me he was afraid he hadn't really changed anyone's life.

Wow. That's quite a confession—especially for a leader. In a melancholy conversation, he grieved about how his life was spent "just holding a bunch of meetings." People liked to hear Ted communicate, but once the engagement was over, he couldn't point to any lasting change he'd catalyzed. He told me he tried to adjust his business model, but it was too little too late. He feared he'd only given people "inspirational goose bumps."

While I'm not sure Ted's evaluation of his life is totally accurate, his confession became a wake-up call for me. I don't want to feel that way or say those kinds of things when I'm through. I don't want to only make a splash.

The Difference?

While I'm not diminishing the value of a good public speaker, I think most of us will admit that mere speaking events don't really change people. Many leaders step onto the platform and simply make a splash. Anyone can do that. Nothing changes.

Real leaders make waves. Splashes energize. Waves catalyze. Splashes entertain. Waves equip. Both are important, but only one genuinely improves performance.

Human Resource executives mourn the reality of this truth. So many have hosted training events on important topics like diversity, teamwork, creativity, or motivation, only to see employees return to their routines afterward. It usually takes time to recognize the only way to have a lasting effect on the people who attend our training events is to establish a plan to discuss and apply what was introduced at the event. This transforms our topics from being fads and us from becoming a flash in the pan.

Let me attempt to summarize the difference between splashes and waves:

SPLASH LEADERS	**WAVE LEADERS**
1. Usually offer glitz and glamor	1. Always offer substance and depth
2. Make noise and gain attention	2. Make a difference and gain retention
3. Make a big first impression on people	3. Foster steady growth in people
4. Contribute to a great event	4. Contribute to a life-changing process
5. Think short-term impact	5. Think long-term influence
6. Big flash overnight	6. Big change over time
7. Transactional	7. Transformational

LET'S TRADE IN GLITZ FOR GROWTH

Unfortunately, we live in a day of events and celebrities. We love the excitement of a huge crowd, with bands, lights, smoke, and great speakers. That will probably always be true. In today's world, however, where it's difficult to "wow" an audience because so many messages compete for our attention, let's remember the power of the wave.

Don't get me wrong. There's nothing wrong with a leader who can make some splashes. We need those who can energize an event and motivate an audience. It's just incomplete. We desperately need leaders who make waves and move people to establish new habits and attitudes. The splash is about glitz. The wave is about growth, and growth usually happens in a developmental relationship with a mentor and some colleagues.

Years ago, the *Harvard Business Review* published a cover article entitled, "Everyone Who Makes It Has a Mentor." The article revealed a study done on hundreds of CEO's across the country: male and female, old and young, and from various ethnicities. Interestingly, their success held no secret, singular formula. The stories were varied. There was, however, one common thread. Each of these leaders reported having a mentor and a community they could talk to in tough times. It was about relationships for them. They all continued in a growth process, which had sparked their success.[10]

Splash leaders spark great moments. Wave leaders spark great movements.

REFLECT AND RESPOND

1. Why do you think people are so drawn to big events and to those who make a big splash?

---

2. List some of the reasons why "wave leaders" have a more difficult job.

_____

_____

3. What are the benefits of becoming a "wave leader?" Why are they life-giving?

_____

_____

Assess Yourself

Reflect on your vocation. Circle the answer that accurately describes you:

When planning training events…

1. I put as much time into preparing for the follow up as I do for the event itself:

   NEVER   **INFREQUENTLY**   **SOMETIMES**   **FREQUENTLY**   **ALWAYS**

2. I care as much about the steady, residual growth of the audience as I do about the immediate response of the audience:

   NEVER   **INFREQUENTLY**   **SOMETIMES**   **FREQUENTLY**   **ALWAYS**

3. I place more value in the results of the event than I do the programming success of the event:

   NEVER   **INFREQUENTLY**   **SOMETIMES**   **FREQUENTLY**   **ALWAYS**

Try it Out: Practicing the Principle

Before your next training event, reflect on how authentic growth usually takes time in plants, animals, humans, and organizations. Then, evaluate the planning of your event in light of these issues:

1. Are you OK with starting small?

2. Can you embrace slow, steady growth?

3. Can you wait for the fruit (results) of your work?

Journal about how you usually measure your success. In the past, have you been more about being a great speaker than prioritizing steady growth from attendees? Take a moment and honestly evaluate your personal style. Share your thoughts with a friend and discuss how you can improve.

The Marathon Problem

EVERY MARATHON HAS PARTICIPANTS AND SPECTATORS. THERE ARE FAR FEWER PEOPLE WHO ACTUALLY RUN IN A MARATHON THAN THERE ARE FANS WHO WATCH THE RACE. THIS IS A PICTURE OF MOST ORGANIZATIONS—A FEW DO MOST OF THE WORK. LIFE-GIVING LEADERS MOBILIZE THE MANY.

You've probably met someone who's run in a marathon. Several cities host them on a yearly basis. The first modern marathon was held in 1896 at the Olympic Games in Athens, Greece. The Boston Marathon started a year later in 1897.

Because it's such a long, brutal race—a little less than twenty-six and a half miles long—not everyone participates in it. There are tens of thousands who watch, but a smaller fraction who actually run the course. In short, there are lots of attendees but fewer participants. At best, those who watch are handing cups of water to the runners to keep them hydrated. They clap, they cheer, they observe—but they don't run.

The same is true for a basketball, baseball or football.

Every game has two components: first, there are a handful players on the field in desperate need of rest. Second, there are thousands of people in the stands in desperate need of exercise. It's true. After all, spectating is so much easier than participating. Players have to put in an incredible amount of work to be out on that field—the fans just show up. It's what I call the marathon problem.

So, why are there far more fans than participants? Oh, there are lots of excuses:

- "I'M NOT GOOD ENOUGH."
- "I'M TOO OLD."
- "I'M TOO YOUNG."
- "I'M NOT FAST ENOUGH."
- "I'M NOT STRONG ENOUGH."
- "YOU'D NEVER WANT ME TO PLAY."
- "I JUST ENJOY WATCHING A GOOD GAME."

Now, consider most non-profit organizations. They often experience the same issue.

Most of them begin with a person—someone who's caught a vision to meet a need. They go after that vision and start meeting that need, which then creates a buzz. The leader collects stories to tell, and soon, others want to jump on board. Sadly, however, most initiatives never get past a handful of people. Organizations generally struggle once they reach a certain point where the central leader can no longer keep his or her finger on the pulse of the action. They often don't want to let go. Doing the work is why they started in the first place. The others who come end up as spectators.

- THEATRE PLAYS
- WORK GROUPS
- MUSIC RECITALS
- CHURCH SERVICES
- CONFERENCES

WHAT HAPPENED TO US?

We live in a day where people are conditioned to be sedentary. We sit to play video games. We sit to watch movies or TV shows. We sit at computers. There is far more sitting than moving in modern culture. It's actually led our population to a significant problem with obesity.

More than that, however, it has fostered a mindset in us. Often, people want their activity to be done while sedentary. We can give to a charitable cause on our phone… while sitting. We can sign a petition online… while sitting. We can shop for clothes or food on the internet… while sitting. In short, we can actually participate (at least a little) while not doing much at all. Some cultural critics have called the emerging generation "slacktivists," which is a combination of "slacker" and "activist." We want to feel like we're changing the world but don't want to move too much in the process. We feel we're active when we're passive, at least physically.

We also live in an era where we're conditioned to watch and critique others. We vote people off a reality TV show. We can criticize others on social media instantly. We post comments on programs we observe; we fire back tweets when we don't like someone without ever having to face them. Life is like a performance. It is an event that most of us watch and judge. The few actually doing the work up front are the "professionals" and the rest of us (the majority) are the "amateurs."

But, this was never how it was supposed to be.

Often, when I talk to young people, they genuinely believe they are not good enough to be the ones leading or serving. They're not active because they don't feel qualified, and they fear failure. So, they never get up and try something. They desperately need the "exercise," but good luck getting them to risk it. They're far too eager to allow the professionals to do it. For too long, we've unwittingly sent and received this message.

What Life Giving Leaders Do

Life-giving leaders get beyond motivating people through financial rewards. They build incentive with more than external stimuli. Life-giving leaders find ways to plug people into appropriate places of active service. They help others "own" the mission. They are mobilizers and catalysts. They build a new mindset into everyone involved:

- The participant stops assuming they must be the only ones to serve.

- The spectators stop assuming they can only watch and begin to serve.

Do you remember the fable of "Stone Soup?" It was about a hungry peasant who entered a village. He asked everyone for a morsel of food, but people said they had nothing to give him. When he looked at their fine homes, he knew it wasn't true. So, he grabbed a large kettle sitting in a field and filled it with water. Then, he invited all the villagers to come see him make a pot of stone soup. This, of course, sounded interesting. When a crowd gathered, he dropped a large stone in the soup, and then tasted it. "Hmmm," he mused. "It's good but something is missing." After a moment, he said, "I know! We need some carrots!" Suddenly, a neighbor exclaimed, "I've got some carrots!" and ran to get them. After dropping the carrots in, he tasted it again and said, "It's better, but I think it needs some potatoes. Does anyone have some?" Smiling, a villager said, "I do!" Again and again, items were added to the soup, until the kettle was full of marvelous, tasty soup—filled by a person who mobilized others who thought they had nothing to give.

For healthy leaders, the goal is to build a pathway for followers to increase their commitment. The path can be described as a "funnel," with many people entering the funnel at the top and (regrettably) fewer actually reaching the bottom. The important thing is that everyone is encouraged to go deeper than mere attendance. The path to commitment is clear. After all, this is not supposed to be a marathon. We want everyone to run.

Funnel Diagram

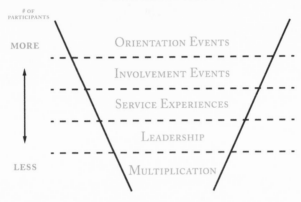

As people enter a team or organization, they generally do so at the top of the funnel. So, events should be designed to attract an entry-level person who's just getting acquainted with your mission or organization. Following the orientation level, are involvement level experiences formed to invite people into deeper relationships and community. Even deeper are service level experiences that invite people to begin using their time and gifts to serve in some way. Further still, are leadership-level experiences that challenge people to grow from serving to actually leading in a particular service area. Finally, the deepest level is the multiplication level where people become leaders of leaders.

You Have to Coach and Train

In order to prepare those you lead for such personal growth and involvement, you must offer training experiences. Otherwise, the average person will never take the plunge. Equipping can be done OJT (On-the-Job Training):

- Watch at first
- Then, you do it together with them
- Later, they do it while you watch
- Finally, they do it while you multiply in someone else

But this process must be intentional. The National FFA Organization (formerly Future Farmers of America) has over 650,000 members. It hosts the largest annual youth convention in the U.S., yet it started with just 33 students in 1928. The Boy Scouts and Girl Scouts are also large organizations that started very small with a handful of people and some kids in 1910 and 1912. Over time, ordinary volunteers became committed, and now, scouting programs boast over 4.2 million members. In every successful case, the growth started when spectators formed a community and became participators.

We must build organizations that organically invite others into...

- ...A CIRCLE, NOT JUST A ROW.
- ...PREPARING FOR SERVICE, NOT JUST A SHOW.
- ...EXPERIENCES THAT MOBILIZE, NOT JUST MOTIVATE.
- ...IDENTIFYING WHAT THEY CAN GIVE, NOT JUST WHAT THEY LIKE TO RECEIVE.

Mission is almost always meant to multiply, to snowball, or accumulate. Everyone qualifies. It's about becoming participants, not spectators, in the marathon.

REFLECT AND RESPOND

1. Where do you see the "marathon problem" occurring today?

_____

_____

2. Why do you think it's harder for leaders to recruit and mobilize volunteers than they first assume?

_____

_____

3. Are you facing any challenges right now that this principle could help solve?

_____

_____

ASSESS YOURSELF

We, as life-giving leaders, must progress through four stages of people development:

- DOING—We do all the work ourselves
- DUMPING—We get frustrated and dump work on others
- DELEGATING—As people avoid our work dumping we learn to plan and delegate tasks
- DEVELOPING—Finally, our ultimate work occurs when we develop others as we offer them ownership of the work

Evaluate yourself. Write down what level you normally operate on, describing what you often do, and the steps you'll take to move people from consumer to contributor.

Review the funnel diagram in this chapter. Do you have sufficient events and outlets for each level? Do you offer enough equipping opportunities to coach people to grow deeper in their participation on your team? Jot down your game plan to build out your own funnel and what training (and encouragement) you could offer those who hope to participate more deeply. What steps will you take to get better? Take a moment and journal about how you'll measure your success.

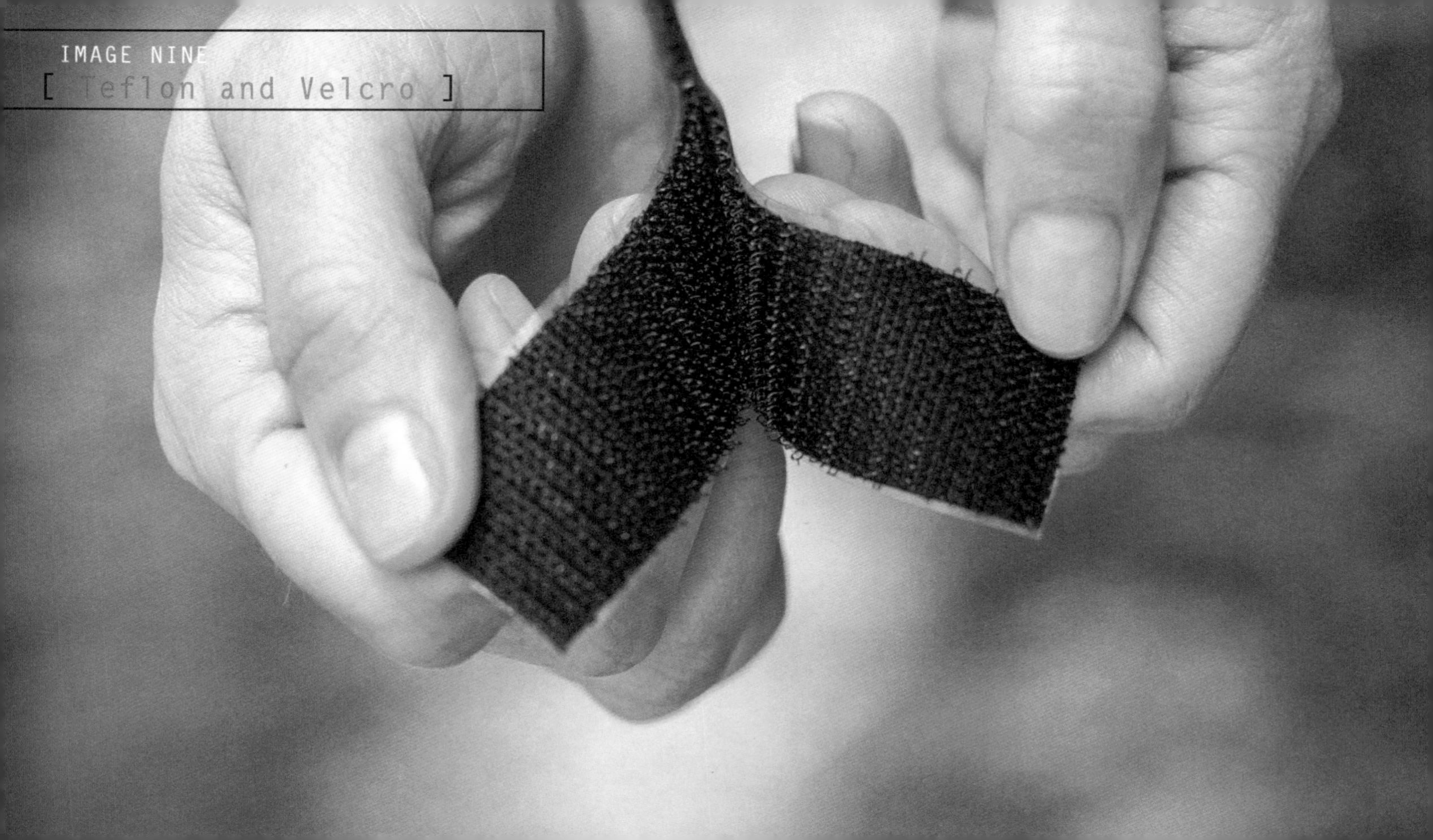

IMAGE NINE
[Teflon and Velcro]

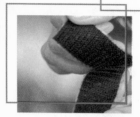

Teflon or Velcro

EVERY LEADER COMMUNICATES, BUT NOT EVERYONE GETS THE MESSAGE THROUGH TO LISTENERS. EFFECTIVE LEADERS ARE LIKE VELCRO. THEY CHOOSE LANGUAGE THAT CONNECTS, STICKS, AND IS NOT QUICKLY FORGOTTEN. THEY USE METAPHORS AND COLORFUL, UNIQUE TERMS THAT TEAM MEMBERS WILL GRASP AND REMEMBER.

I bet you've used pots made of Teflon as well as fabric that includes Velcro. Both are pretty common in today's world. Perhaps you'll enjoy a little background. Modern non-stick pans are usually coated with Teflon (polytetrafluoroethylene or PTFE). Roy Plunkett discovered it spontaneously in 1938, when he worked on a project with the DuPont Company. Believe it or not, the substance was first used in the development of the atomic bomb during World War II. It was valuable because of its unique corrosion-resistant properties.

By 1951, DuPont was solving some chemical problems with Teflon so that it could be used for other purposes as well. Soon, it was primed for discovery. A few years later, Marc Gregoire, a French engineer, was coating his fishing gear with Teflon, when his wife suggested using it to coat her pots and pans. A cookware revolution was about to take place. The Tefal Company was launched in 1956 to manufacture these non-stick pans.

Pretty slick, huh?

Velcro, on the other hand, was invented by a man name George de Mestral in the 1940s while hunting in the Jura Mountains of Switzerland. George was a Swiss engineer who discovered the tiny hooks of the Cockle Burs were getting stuck on his trousers and in his dog's fur. He studied them to discover how they attached themselves so well. Shortly afterward, he re-created the hooks with nylon material that made two fabrics stick. He called his invention Velcro—a combination of the words "velvet" and "crochet"—and formally patented it in 1955. Now, it's everywhere.

Pretty catchy, huh?

How Does This Inform our Leadership?

In short, Teflon is known for being slick so that nothing sticks. Velcro is known for being textured so that everything sticks. In the same way, a leader's communication will either stick with those they lead long after they've spoken, or it'll be forgettable. They'll either have "hooks" for team members to grab onto and remember, or they'll be ideas that fail to attach to anyone. They will slip from their memories.

We've all experienced both, haven't we? Reflect on times when people have spoken to you. Can you remember leaders who droned on and on, using loads of words, yet, it's hard to remember any of them? Conversely, can you recall leaders who find ways to grab listeners with their words and embed them into their minds and hearts? One is Teflon. The other is Velcro.

Now the important question is: which best describes your communication?

Growing up, I remember watching Dr. Martin Luther King, Jr. give speeches on TV. News programs would show clips of him speaking after a civil rights march or demonstration. He always had a way of crystallizing his thoughts into a memorable idea for listeners. He chose his words carefully and left people thinking every time he spoke. He inspired us. His words breathed life into his listeners. Dr. King found ways to make his ideas stick like Velcro.

The Ideas of Life-Giving Leaders Are Velcro Not Teflon

One tangible way leaders can be life giving is through our messaging. What and how do we communicate? Do we breathe life into others with our words? Or, are our words empty and fail to accomplish our intent?

Each of us receives over 10,000 messages each day, via social media, conversations, email, TV, radio, phone calls, and advertising. Take a moment to consider this. It's enough to exhaust me just thinking about it! As a result of this onslaught, teen attention spans have gone from 12 seconds in 2000 to 6-8 seconds today. Herbert Simon summarized the issue when he said, "A wealth of information creates a poverty of attention."[11] So, how do life-giving leaders break through the noise and enable their messages to stand out?

A Velcro Leader's Words Are:

1. Fresh—They are unique
Life-giving leaders find ways to share ideas—even old ideas—in distinctive ways. They find words and mannerisms that are fresh and current for their listeners. It's the difference between the usual, "Good job today," and the stark, "You were excellent leading that meeting. You were clear with the objectives and kept the conversation on track in the midst of lots of different opinions. Well done!"

2. Inspiring—They empower

To be life-giving, by definition, implies inspiration. The words spur others on to higher levels of performance. The key? Inspiration always follows aspiration. People are stimulated when your request is tied to a goal they aspire to reach. Former Prime Minister Winston Churchill always connected his challenge for the British people to sacrifice during World War II to their aspiration of living free from Nazi occupation.

3. Emotional—They connect with the heart

Great communication includes three elements: logos, ethos, and pathos. Logos is about the message itself. Ethos involves the credibility of the speaker. Pathos is an appeal to emotion, persuading listeners through the speakers' passion. It's the fire inside us. Dr. King's speeches included all three—they're logical, emotional, and embodied by Dr. King himself.

4. Clear—They offer specific direction

Messages that are full of passion but don't offer clear direction miss the mark. The motivation is temporary at best, failing to furnish what's needed to hit targets. Clarity brings energy. Clarity brings creativity. Clarity brings resources to listeners. In most political elections, the winner is the one whose message and vision was clearest.

5. Transferrable—They are easy to share

Life-giving leaders utilize words, phrases, and imagery that are memorable and easy for listeners to pass along to others afterward. In fact, great messages are a paradox: they are sticky yet sharable. You keep them but can give them away. Think about TV commercials you still remember. I bet their message is both sticky and sharable.

6. Timely—They are relevant

I believe messages that stick the best are tied to what listeners are facing in the moment. Life-giving leaders are privy to current events, in tune with the feelings of listeners, and deliver words that are both timely and timeless for audiences to implement.

When I created the first *Habitudes* images, I tried to follow the rules of effective, life giving communication. The chapters are short and to the point. They're driven by an image, which touches the heart, not just the head, and makes the principle sticky. In short, our communication has a better chance of influencing people today if it is short, simple, sticky, and shareable.

Two Case Studies

A simple study was done on motivating kids. On Halloween night, researchers placed a bowl of apples on a doorstep next to a bowl of candy. In between them, a sign read: "You ought to take an apple." After a sampling of trick-or-treaters, researchers found the vast majority of kids took the candy. It was predictable.

Children love candy.

Once the sign was changed, however, nearly half the kids took an apple. What did the new sign say?

It simply read: "What would Batman eat?"

Instead of communicating "obligation" the message was about "inspiration." It was an appeal to the child's aspiration—to be like batman. The same principle applies to life-giving leaders. Their messages are Velcro because they speak to the heart and hope of their listeners. They tie inspiration to aspiration.

Following the Battle of Gettysburg, two leaders offered speeches in memory of the soldiers who'd died in that Civil War conflict. Edward Everett gave a two-hour speech, and Abraham Lincoln offered a 2-3 minute speech. Afterward, Everett perceived Lincoln's life-giving words. He wrote Lincoln, praising him for his eloquent and concise speech, saying, "I should be glad if I could flatter myself that I came as near to the central idea of the occasion in two hours as you did in two minutes."

In reality, the speech contained 272 words, and took Lincoln 2-3 minutes to give. But we still memorize them today. I have no idea what Mr. Everett said in his speech.

It reminds me of *Velcro and Teflon*.

REFLECT AND RESPOND

1. Why are these "Velcro communicators" so rare?

   _____

   _____

2. Can you recall a "Velcro message" given by a life-giving leader? Who and when?

   _____

   _____

3. What circumstances make it difficult for you to be a Velcro communicator?

   _____

   _____

ASSESS YOURSELF

Evaluate your communication based on two grids below. Reflect on a central message you try to relay to others, and see if you include these important elements:

1. **LOGOS**: What's the content of your message?

_____

_____

2. **ETHOS**: Do you have the credibility to give it?

_____

_____

3. **PATHOS**: Do you have genuine passion about it?

_____

_____

In order to foster life change, life-giving leaders usually include three things in their message:

1. A **POINT** for their head. What's the key idea?

_____

_____

2. A **PICTURE** for their heart. Can you illustrate it?

_____

_____

3. **PRACTICE** for their hands. What's an action step?

_____

_____

Try it Out: Practicing the Principle

Plan to practice the following changes as you interact with others this week:

1. Don't think **obligation**, think *inspiration*.
   Instead of telling people they ought to do something, why not inspire them to hit a target because they want to? Tie your words to their aspirations.

2. Don't think **descriptive**, think *prescriptive*.
   Instead of telling people every step to take toward an outcome, why not describe the outcome together and let them figure out the steps?

3. Don't think **inform**, think *interpret*.
   People don't need leaders for information, but for interpretation. Instead of being an informer, help them interpret how to think, not what to think.

4. Don't think **impose**, think *expose*.
   No one wants to do something if they're forced to do so. Why not expose them to opportunities and let them choose to jump in on them?

5. Don't think **control**, think *connect*.
   As i mentioned before, control is a myth. Why not seek connection with others at the heart level to influence them instead of trying to control them.

Fountains and Drains

LEADERS ARE USUALLY A FOUNTAIN OR A DRAIN—THEY FLOW AND OVERFLOW
ONTO OTHERS, OR THEY JUST DRAIN PEOPLE OF THEIR ENERGY. THEY EITHER
REFRESH THE LIFE IN OTHERS... OR THEY DRY IT UP. DRIVEN BY GRATITUDE AND
PERSPECTIVE, LIFE-GIVING LEADERS FOCUS ON EMPOWERING PEOPLE RATHER
THAN EXPLOITING THEM.

You and I have experienced both fountains and drains over the years. Both have
to do with water flow. The big difference? One is about water flowing upward
or outward, perhaps in a city square or a garden. These are fountains. They are
beautiful to see. They carry with them a positive connotation. They are flowing
expressions of life that people love to watch and admire. Some of the most
attractive places to visit have fountains positioned in a prominent place.

Drains, on the other hand, are about water flowing downward. They are an opening
in the sink that sends water, and anything else in that basin, down the plumbing,
through the pipes, and into the sewer. It's a rather gross picture. They often carry
a negative connotation with them. We talk about "draining experiences" or people
who "drain us of our energy." They are the opposite of fountains.

What's interesting is that both exist in that garden or city square. Every fountain
that people take pictures of above the ground also has a drain below the surface of
the water. You just can't see it, and the architects planned it that way. No one ever
comes to look at a drain. They come to view a fountain.

My early years were spent in Cincinnati, Ohio. From time to time, my family
would visit Fountain Square in the heart of the city. It was eye-catching. A large
statue stands high in the middle and has flowing water streaming down on two
sides. People would come and toss coins in the pool at its base, making a wish as
they threw it in. Built in 1871, Fountain Square remains as a landmark in that
downtown area. While I've visited it many times over the years, and I assumed it
was always there, I never remember once looking for the drain.

This is a picture of leadership and teams.

Many leaders are like fountains. They flow and overflow into the lives of others...
and because they do, they're attractive to people. When this leader's life touches

another person, it is energizing. It is encouraging. It sparks new ideas. It makes people feel better. They are life giving. Dynamic. Satisfying. They overflow with appreciation for others. When you see a fountain leader, you immediately want to be around them.

Other leaders are more like drains. They're always preoccupied with what's wrong with their team or what they don't have or still need—and they drain the energy out of people. In fact, when you see these people coming, you tend to try and avoid them. They'll sap you of your optimism. They'll deplete your energy for trying new ideas with fifty reasons why they won't work.

In short, fountains are water going up. Drains are water going down. So, how do people move from being a "drain" to a "fountain?"

IT'S ABOUT OUR APPROACH TO LEADERSHIP

It all begins with perspective. Team members who are fountains focus on gratitude for what they have. They never lose sight of what others have done for them; they know they didn't make it this far in life alone. They're thankful for opportunities, mindful of helpful people, and spill that gratitude and optimism onto others.

Team members who are drains tend to see the darker side of life. They reflect on the past and have regrets for what might have been. They focus on missed opportunities or failures. Life seems scarce rather than abundant. They're consumed with fears, doubts, or shame and tend to drain others of energy.

Research done with people both young and old reveals very interesting conclusions on the role of gratitude. Author and researcher Dr. Robert Emmons of the University of California Davis believes he knows what gives life meaning: pure and simple gratitude.

Emmons' team found that people who view life as a gift and consciously acquire an "attitude of gratitude" experience multiple advantages. Gratitude improves emotional and physical health and can strengthen relationships, communities, and teams. Some strategies to build gratitude include keeping a gratitude journal, learning poems and quotes about gratitude, and using visual reminders.

"Without gratitude, life can be lonely, depressing, and impoverished," Emmons said. "Gratitude enriches human life. It elevates, energizes, inspires, and transforms. People are moved, opened, and humbled through expressions of gratitude."[12]

Unfortunately, cultivating an attitude of gratitude isn't easy.

The Inverse Relationship Between Gratitude and Entitlement

Gratitude is, according to Emmons, a "chosen attitude." We must be willing to recognize that we are the recipients of an unearned benefit. This is especially rare today where social media encourages us to build quite a narcissistic worldview. We live in a culture that cultivates a sense of entitlement, and it's seen across generations.

Do you ever find yourself feeling like you deserve any good you receive? It has happened to me too. I've realized I have to fight against that sense of entitlement each day because it's contrary to the growth of a spirit of gratitude. Entitlement is virtually the opposite of gratitude: as I feel more entitled, my gratitude shrinks in proportion.

Research indicates that gratitude is not merely a positive emotion—it can improve your health, if cultivated. Research also indicates that people must give up a "victim mentality" and overcome a sense of entitlement. Think for a moment. When someone feels entitled to benefits, there's little need for gratitude: I don't need to thank anyone; I deserved the gift. In fact, these people are lucky to have me around. I'm amazing.

As I have studied emerging leaders and their struggles, I've found that gratitude can actually have a positive impact on so many areas of their growth: energy levels, motivation, mental well-being, academic achievement, healthy, lasting relationships, and dealing with tragedy and crisis. Why would anyone not want to adopt this mindset?

In one study, researchers had participants test a number of different gratitude exercises such as thinking about a living person for whom they were grateful, writing about someone for whom they were grateful, or writing a letter to deliver to someone for whom they were grateful. Other participants were merely asked to describe a room in their house (the neutral group). Participants who engaged in a gratitude exercise showed increases in positive emotion immediately after the exercise. In people who become habitually grateful, negative events have little influence on their gratitude (McCullough, Tsang & Emmons, 2004). Gratitude becomes a state of mind or a way of living.

In our work with professional sports teams, we enjoy our partnership with the Kansas City Royals. General Manager Dayton Moore called up Salvador "Salvi" Perez to the major leagues in 2011. At a press conference, Perez was asked why he didn't demand more money in his contract. The moment grew a little tense as Dayton was sitting on the same panel. But, I loved the way Perez responded. He smiled and said, "I'm just grateful to play on this team and help build a winning club." That's the spirit that earned him a World Series MVP and helped the Royals win the World Series in 2015.

Athletes who appreciate their teammates are contagious. Sadly, those who are only into themselves, their playing time, their stats, and their social media platform become drains, and yes, that kind of negativity also tends to be contagious.

How to Become a Fountain

The good news is that each of us has the opportunity to be "fountain" teammates and leaders. We can become "problem solvers," instead of "problem finders." Here are seven elements "fountain leaders" possess:

- Energy—Even when quiet, they exude passion that energizes others
- Empathy—They can identify and feel what others are experiencing
- Optimism—They are hopeful and see the bright side of every issue
- Generosity—Their abundance mindset enables them give what they have
- Selflessness—They see the big picture and serve others before themselves
- Empowerment—They are confident and believe in others' potential
- Encouragement—They offer words that give courage to those around them

Does anything influence you more than gratitude — negative conditions, bad attitudes, addictions or regret? Are people energized or drained by you?

Drain Leaders	Fountain Leaders
1. Discouraging to people	1. Encouraging to people
2. See the downside of problems	2. See the upside of opportunities
3. Live with doubts and pessimism	3. Live by faith and optimism
4. Motivate through guilt	4. Motivated through gratitude
5. People feel they don't measure up	5. People feel they can reach big goals
6. Source of caution and fear	6. Source of life and possibilities
7. Driven by memories	7. Driven by dreams

Two men were lying in hospital beds, both with terminal diseases. One bed was next to a window; the other rested further inside the room and kept the patient from seeing out of the window. As the two men talked each day, the man by the window would smile as he shared what he could see looking out the window. He described a park with kids playing on a swing set, an ice cream vendor serving families a cold treat, and lovers strolling along the sidewalk. This made him happy. In fact, each day, the man inside the room grew resentful that he wasn't able to see these things. Why couldn't he be next to that window? One day, the man by the window passed away in his sleep. After he was removed from the room, his angry roommate asked to be moved to the bed next to the window. When he was, he got the surprise of his life. He gazed out the window and found that it faced a blank wall.

REFLECT AND RESPOND

1. Why do you think people tend to grow negative instead of positive about life?

_____

_____

2. When you think about the team you are a part of or are leading, what habits could create a "fountain" culture instead of a "drain" culture?

_____

_____

3. What have you done to cultivate an attitude of gratitude yourself?

_____

_____

ASSESS YOURSELF

Take a candid look at your leadership style. Then, place an "X" on the point in the line that best describes your leadership:

1. When a problem arises, would people expect me to react with…

|--|

HOPEFUL SOLUTIONS   **RESENTFUL BLAME**

2. When interacting with people in conversation, I tend to…

|--|

CONTRIBUTE ENERGY   **CONSUME ENERGY**

3. When examining a program or project, I usually…

|--|

SEE WHAT'S WRONG   **RECOGNIZE WHAT'S WRONG**

TRY IT OUT: PRACTICING THE PRINCIPLE

Always remember—we do need to see problems as they arise and spot the negative impact of our mistakes when present. Leaders often need to be the ones who "drain" a program of what's wrong. However, seeing the upside of things usually breeds a contagious appreciative spirit. This week, make an extra effort to see the bright side in every interaction you have with people. Then, consider the fellow students, teammates or coworkers who help make "good things happen" in your life.

Next, find a way to communicate your gratitude. You can meet with them, write them a note, or make a phone call and acknowledge how thankful you are for them. Finally, ask yourself, "What could I do or say that would make people grateful I'm on their team?" Identify specific ways you could be a "fountain" for others and practice being this type of leader. Talk them over the next time you meet together.

Culture and Customs

LIFE-GIVING LEADERS KNOW THE BEST WAY TO BUILD A TEAM EVERYONE WANTS TO BE A PART OF IS BY CREATING THE RIGHT CULTURE. WHY? BECAUSE OUR CONTEXT ALWAYS EXPLAINS OUR CONDUCT. GOOD LEADERS GROW THEIR CULTURE BY FOSTERING SUSTAINABLE CUSTOMS, STRONG VALUES, AND CLEAR LANGUAGE.

I bet you've traveled to another country. At this point in my life, I've trained leaders in fifty countries around the world and always enjoy learning something while I am there. From industrialized nations like England and Singapore to developing nations like Uganda and Sri Lanka, I usually enter with expectations and exit with lessons learned from the variety of ethnic groups on Earth.

One particular lesson has been especially helpful over the years. When I see someone behave in a certain fashion, I've come to understand there's usually a good reason for it. While we are all part of the human race, we come from different ethnic groups, backgrounds, paradigms, and environments.

For years, I've wondered why so many of the fastest runners in international competitions are from Kenya. For instance, at the 2011 World Track and Field Championships, Kenya won an incredible 17 medals in the middle and long distance running events. The U.S. only won three. In marathon running, Kenyans are even more dominant. In 2011, the world's top 20 fastest runners—in the world's most universal and accessible sport—were all from Kenya. Something is going on there in the Rift Valley, where most of Kenya's runners originate. So, what is it? It's context.

Virtually every successful Kenyan runner is from a poor, rural family. From an early age, they have to run everywhere. Daniel Komen, the world record holder for the 3000 m. race said, "Every day I used to milk the cows, run to school, run home for lunch, back to school, home, tend the cows. This is the Kenyan way."[13]

As I've visited dozens of countries, I have found that not only do cultures differ from each other, but those cultures vividly illuminated me as to why people behave the way they do. Some cultures are naturally happy, while others are more depressed; some are very passionate and expressive, while others are more quiet. Some are calculated, precise, and time oriented and others are more relational, warm, and event oriented. I am not arguing that any people group is better than another. They are just different based on the culture in which they live.

CONTEXT EXPLAINS CONDUCT

The truth is, when people act a certain way, the environment around them generally fosters that behavior. Severe circumstances actually induce behavior. In short: context explains conduct. All human behavior has a reason behind it. Behavior is always solving a problem—whether in a healthy or unhealthy way. People act to ease their pain, to get an answer, to meet a need, or to resolve a dilemma. In fact, crime is often an attempt to meet a real need in an unhealthy way. The sooner leaders understand this fact, the better off we will be. It doesn't excuse bad behavior, but it does explain it.

A therapist once told me about a family she was counseling. The parents brought their six-year-old son in for an appointment because they were sure he had mental health issues. When they'd leave the house for any reason, the boy would become emotional and scream. He often withdrew from social settings and hide in the bathroom. He came out smelling awful, as if he'd wiped his urine or excrement on his body. After careful conversation, the therapist met with the parents and gave a diagnosis. The boy was not crazy. He had been abused when they visited his uncle and believed the only solution was to hide or become so repulsive, no one would touch him.

A tragic illustration of the fact that context explains conduct.

WHAT CONTEXT ARE YOU CREATING?

My question for you is this: when you look at the behavior of the people you are leading, what does it say about your own leadership? What does it say about the context that you've created?

Effective life-giving leaders prioritize the cultivation of a healthy context and culture in their organizations. Knowing that conduct stems from context, they create the right environment for each person to experience health because healthy things naturally grow. For years, I have appreciated the statement, "When a flower doesn't bloom, you fix the environment in which it grows, not the flower."

The context of your leadership is made up of two ingredients: your systems and culture. When an organization isn't healthy, there's usually a failure of one of these two things.

1. SYSTEMS—The processes you put in place to get things done. Systems are all about maximizing peoples' gifts and capacity to achieve their goals.
2. CULTURE—The atmosphere you cultivate to foster energy. Culture is all about peoples' growth and engagement in the mission.

In short, systems are about efficiency. Culture is about engagement. When your context isn't bearing fruit, you can almost always bank on the fact that you have failed to create an effective system and/or culture.

The Power of Culture on a Team of People:

- All teams have a culture, by default or design.
- People are carriers of culture, good or bad.
- Some teammates are more contagious than others.
- There are as many cultures as there are managers.
- The culture affects behavior more than anything else.
- Leaders must hire the culture they want in team members.
- There is a difference between culture and climate.
- A leader's job is to cultivate a healthy culture.
- They do this through their habits and attitudes.
- Effective leaders know that people ultimately do what they see.

Kennesaw Mountain High School is a poignant example of how culture can affect everyone. Years ago, the leaders decided they needed to start an anti-bullying campaign and foster a culture of leadership within the student body. As a result, they not only experienced a greater acceptance among diverse student populations, but also students began launching programs that changed lives.

One group hosted a prom for special needs students where the athletes, cheerleaders, and student leaders adopted the invitees at this dance and hosted them like royalty. The facility, the food, and the decorations were all paid for by the money raised by students for their special peers. The culture of the school has transformed so dramatically over the years that local businesses have told me they seek to hire graduates from KMHS because they understand that school is producing profoundly mature leaders. Kennesaw has become an incubator for leaders. Why? It's simple. They transformed the context, and context is what cultivates great people.

What All Cultures Share

In the "Assess Yourself" section of this chapter, you'll have the chance to evaluate the kind of culture you've experienced in the past. For now, I'd like to discuss three elements every culture shares. Reflect for a moment. When you visit another nation, you usually discover how different they are through the following elements:

1. Shared Values
In Peru, for instance, they value relationships more than time. It's not as important to start a meeting on time as it is to connect with others. In the U.S., while relationships are important, we prioritize punctuality. Different values.

What are your values?

2. Shared Customs

In England, people drive cars on the left-hand side of the road. In America, we drive on the right side. Neither side is better, they're just different customs. All countries have certain customs or traditions that perpetuate the culture.

What are your customs?

3. Shared Language

This one is obvious. In France, people speak French. In Germany, they speak German. Each country has a primary language (or languages) used to connect and communicate. This, too, perpetuates the culture, values, and lifestyle. Companies, schools, and organizations also have certain words and phrases commonly used that reveal their organizational culture.

What is your language?

These are the elements that create context—on accident or on purpose. We must remember that the context of a place will explain the conduct of its people. And climate may change daily.

Context explains conduct.

REFLECT AND RESPOND

1. What have you learned from visiting another culture? Can you think of an example of something that seemed really different to you, but once you learned the back story and saw it in the context, it became something you could value and appreciate?

   _____

   _____

2. If you could describe the culture of the best team you have ever been a part of, what words would you use to describe that team's values, customs, and language?

   _____

   _____

3. In what ways have you seen a leader set the tone for a culture of a class, team, or organization?

   _____

   _____

Assess Yourself

Organizations experience a variety of cultures that can diminish the potential of a team. Look over the list of organizational cultures below and determine if you have experienced any of these "less than optimal" environments. Place an X on the dotted line to accurately communicate how much you've witnessed them.

Description	Your Experience
Toxic Negativity sabotages relationships, trust, and results.	NO ----------------- YES
Distant People are guarded, superficial, and only go the first mile.	NO ----------------- YES
Fun Great context, but you wonder, "Are we productive here?"	NO ----------------- YES
Confused Staff goal is to look busy; team is not aligned or focused.	NO ----------------- YES
Stagnant Maintenance, not mission is the team goal—plateaued.	NO ----------------- YES
Stagnant Folks wander unsure and shoot themselves in the foot.	NO ----------------- YES

Try it Out: Practicing the Principle

This week practice asking "why" whenever you see someone do something you don't understand. When appropriate, ask them why they acted as they did. Journal what you discover from their answers. This simple exercise is eye-opening to most leaders. Discuss your observations with your team.

IMAGE TWELVE

[Stethoscopes and Treatments]

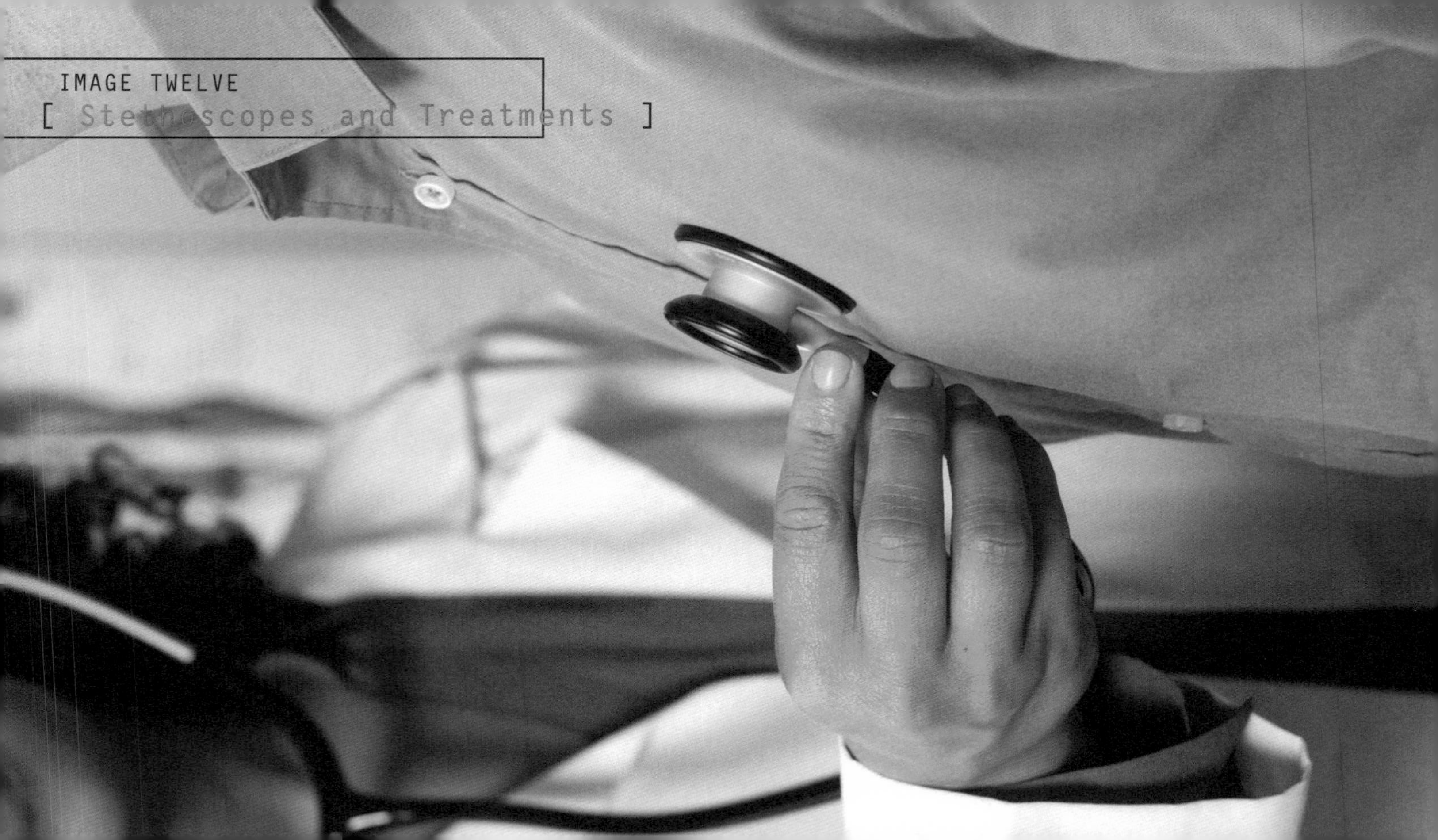

Stethoscopes and Treatments

BEFORE PRESCRIBING TREATMENT, DOCTORS ALWAYS DIAGNOSE A PATIENT BY USING A STETHOSCOPE AND OTHER TOOLS TO LISTEN TO THEIR PATIENT'S HEART. LIFE-GIVING LEADERS APPROACH PEOPLE THE SAME WAY—THEY READ THEM BEFORE THEY LEAD THEM.

I'm sure you've made a few trips to the doctor's office in your past. As a Type 1 diabetic, I make several of them each year. I'll never forget getting diagnosed with diabetes in the fall of 1980. I was in college, and everything was going well. I was making good grades, playing sports, had some great friends, and served in a number of off-campus service projects. But that year, my body began doing some strange things. I became tired and thirsty all the time. I could hardly walk up a flight of stairs without stopping to rest. Then, my vision started going blurry. At that point, my roommate insisted I see a doctor.

It was then I got the news—my pancreas had stopped working. I was sent to the hospital and began taking insulin injections for my high blood sugars.

Along the way, I noticed the steps my doctors always took as they examined me. They'd look me over—my mouth, my eyes, and my ears. Then, they'd put a stethoscope up to my heart. Only after observing and listening did they prescribe a treatment.

I recently spoke to a doctor who told me he was taught in medical school to take at least ten minutes to diagnose someone before drawing any conclusions. In other words, good doctors read people before they lead people.

THE STETHOSCOPE OF A LIFE-GIVING LEADER

I believe good leaders follow the same path. They don't merely bark out orders for their team. Even when they know what steps must be taken, they take time to listen and to observe what's happening in the minds of their team members. Just like a doctor who already knows her patient likely needs an antibiotic, she'll still take the time to listen before speaking and observe before diagnosing.

One of the reasons this is necessary is because people send verbal and non-verbal messages to each other, and these messages all contain some subtext. Facial expressions often relay emotions. Body language communicates disposition. People tend to bring their personal lives with them to work. Good leaders function like a doctor, meaning that they lead after determining the backstory. They seek to understand before being understood. Just knowing that a person's behavior stems from both environments and temperament gives us insight. It's like using a stethoscope before deciding on a treatment.

THEIR BEHAVIOR SHOULD INFORM OUR BEHAVIOR

In the last *Habitude*, "Culture and Customs", I explained that context explains conduct. The sooner leaders understand this principle, the better. In addition, this means we must choose our approach based on whom we are leading. Like good doctors, we must be able to "diagnose" our "patients." Wise leaders lead with empathy. We must feel, not just think, as we lead. And we lead based upon who they are, not just who we are.

Why is this necessary for effective leadership?

Empathy has been defined as the capacity to understand or feel what another person is experiencing from within the other person's frame of reference. It is the capacity to place oneself in another's position. There are many definitions for empathy that encompass a broad range of emotional states. However, for this *Habitude*, we will stick to three main types of empathy:

- COGNITIVE EMPATHY—THE CONSCIOUS DRIVE TO UNDERSTAND SOMEONE'S EMOTIONAL STATE
- EMOTIONAL EMPATHY—THE NATURAL DRIVE TO RESPOND ACCURATELY TO SOMEONE'S STATE
- SOMATIC EMPATHY—THE MUTUAL PROCESS OF BOTH PEOPLE MIRRORING THEIR EMOTIONS

In many ways, empathy is the opposite of apathy, which is to feel nothing. Pathos, a root word connected to apathy, is about passion. Apathy is about lacking passion. Life-giving leaders not only sense passion for their team's mission, but they feel it for their people.

"Having empathy also includes having the understanding that there are many factors that go into decision making and cognitive thought processes," Cindy Dietrich wrote. "Past experiences have an influence on decision making today. Understanding this allows a person to have empathy for individuals who sometimes make illogical decisions … Broken homes, childhood trauma, lack of parenting and other factors can influence the connections in the brain which a person uses to make decisions."

IN SHORT, WHEN LEADERS HAVE EMPATHY, THEY LEAD PEOPLE OUT OF A DEEP DISCERNMENT OF THE FACTORS GOING INTO EACH INTERACTION. THEY LEAD BEYOND LOGIC.

CASE STUDY OF AN EMPATHETIC LEADER

I'll never forget reading about Lieutenant Colonel Christopher Hughes. He was a commander of the 2nd Battalion, 327th infantry regiment in Iraq in 2003. When his battalion received a shipment of food and supplies for the Iraqi people, Hughes decided the best place to distribute it was the local mosque. So, he and his troops marched toward the house of the local cleric, the Grand Ayatollah Ali al-Sistani, to ask if he'd like to oversee the distribution. As the soldiers marched, however, locals assumed they were going to kidnap the cleric or bomb the mosque. A crowd gathered to stop the soldiers with sticks and rocks in their hands, ready for a fight. Two started throwing rocks at the soldiers. It was a tense moment.

That's when Hughes led with emotional intelligence and lots of empathy. He instructed his armed soldiers to stop, to drop down on one knee, to point their guns toward the ground and to look up into the eyes of the local Iraqis and smile. One by one, the locals began dropping their stones, and eventually, they smiled right back. Hughes avoided a conflict by leading with empathy rather than force.

Over my career, I have witnessed the disarming power of empathetic leaders. While they may appear to some as weak, they're actually strong. They display the strength to read a situation and do what is needed to make progress. In fact, I have come to believe these truths about our leadership approach:

1. There is not just one right way to lead.
Over the decades, universities that study leadership have evolved in their thinking. Good leadership is not reserved for the driven personality type that takes charge of the room. There are many effective approaches to leadership.

2. Effective leaders will change their style but not their principles.
Life-giving leaders know what can change and what must not change. Principles that make teams work are timeless: integrity, discipline, clear communication, vision, etc. However, our approach to a situation is based on whom we lead, when we lead, where we lead, and why we lead.

3. Lasting leaders choose their style by observing their people.
This is why successful, life-giving leaders are adaptable. Empathy—or reading the people and the situation first—informs the approach they take. After listening and observing the people around them, they wisely choose a relevant style.

Not only does context explain people's conduct, it should explain ours as well.

The Stethoscope of a Life-Giving Leader

Years ago, author Stephen Covey taught us that effective leaders "seek to understand before being understood."[14] For this reason, doctors take time to diagnose before treating a patient. As life-giving leaders, our methods should look much like theirs:

- Show me your eyes—What have you seen or experienced?

- Show me your ears—What have you heard that informs your behavior?

- Let me see your mouth—What do the words you have spoken reveal to me?

- Let me listen to your heart—What's going on inside that helps me understand?

- Where does it hurt—What pain (lack) do you feel that helps me to lead you well?

Years ago, I met an NCAA coach who grumbled at his young athletes who had little grit or stamina and felt entitled to perks beyond their scholarship. What's more, when he'd yell at them to toughen them up, they withdrew. They couldn't seem to take his shouting. He assumed they were wimps. During our discussion, however, we looked at the backgrounds of most of his young athletes. Until then, they'd always been the best on their team, they were seldom yelled at, and they were consistently told they were excellent, just for participating. While this did not get them ready for adulthood or college athletics, it did explain their actions. It also helped the coach develop a better approach for coaching his players.

The next season, he learned that when he began with empathy and then moved to expectations, he got the results he wanted. It required him, however, to seek to understand before being understood.

Too often, we fail to seek understanding and jump into the treatment, much like an incompetent doctor who rushes in to see a patient—without their stethoscope. The longer I've been a leader, the easier it is for me to make this same mistake. I've mastered my work, forgetting how hard it was to learn it. I feel confident; I have answers and assume I know what team members are feeling. Sadly, I can forget the basics of relationships.

Katy was a young girl who asked her father if she could play at her neighbor's house one afternoon. Her dad said yes but told her to return by 6 p.m. for dinner. When Katy strutted in the house thirty minutes late, her dad asked for an explanation. She simply said that her friend's doll broke. Her dad asked if she had been helping her friend fix the broken doll.

"No," Katy explained. "I was helping her cry."

Reflect and Respond

1. Why do leaders fail to practice this principle? What makes empathy hard?

   _____

   _____

2. When is it most difficult for you to use your "stethoscope" to better understand others? Are some personalities or situations harder for you than others?

   _____

   _____

3. Can you think of a time when you saw a leader demonstrate empathy? What was the outcome?

   _____

   _____

Assess Yourself

Circle the most accurate description of your leadership:

1. When team members fail to comprehend directions, I tend to...

   - GET IMPATIENT WITH THEM
   - FEEL SYMPATHY FOR THEM
   - BECOME DISTANT AROUND THEM
   - IMPROVE MY COMMUNICATION

2. If a teammate comes late to a meeting, I usually...

   - ASSUME THEY DON'T TAKE JOBS SERIOUSLY
   - WONDER IF ANYTHING IS WRONG
   - THINK THEY'RE UNDISCIPLINED OR UNREADY
   - ASK IF THEY'RE ALRIGHT

3. When a team member fails at a project, the first thing I think is...

   - "THEY'RE INCOMPETENT."
   - "HAVE I FAILED TO LEAD THEM WELL?"
   - "I PICKED THE WRONG PERSON."
   - "I'VE MADE MISTAKES IN THE PAST."

Try it Out: Practicing the Principle

According to Martin Hoffman, a psychologist who studied empathy development, everyone is born capable of feeling empathy. Unfortunately, not all leaders possess an equal amount of it.[15] Each day this week, enter your conversations with an imaginary stethoscope in hand. Ask questions and listen to peoples' hearts before assuming anything or giving directions. Jot down how others react. Discuss it.

The Golden Gate Paradox

AFTER A NET WAS PLACED UNDER THE BUILDERS OF THE GOLDEN GATE BRIDGE, CONSTRUCTION WAS FINISHED QUICKLY. LEADERS MUST BE DISPENSERS OF GRACE, ALLOWING TEAM MEMBERS TO FAIL FORWARD. THIS ENABLES TEAM MEMBERS TO SUCCEED MORE OFTEN AND MORE QUICKLY.

The building of the Golden Gate Bridge was a stunning feat in engineering. Bridge construction began in 1933, in the midst of the Great Depression. The unemployment rate was 25 percent, so people were looking for jobs. With the exception of some very specialized tasks, the bridge was built almost entirely by a local labor force. Workers were proud to be part of one of the most incredible achievements of the industrial revolution.

What you may not know is that the building of the Golden Gate Bridge is a story of astonishing safety standards. The expectation at the time for steel bridge construction during that time was one fatality for every $1 million in cost. By those standards, the safety record for the Golden Gate Bridge was impressive— losing only 11 workers for the $35 million project. How did they pull this off?

Typically, when someone fell and died during a bridge's construction, work actually slowed down because the remaining workers became apprehensive and fearful. Deadlines were missed, as the men became preoccupied with survival rather than success.

Chief Engineer Joseph Strauss was convinced, however, that although deadlines might be missed, workers needed to labor safely. So, Strauss made the site the first in America to have a $130,000 safety net suspended underneath the construction. The net saved the lives of 19 workers who called themselves the "Halfway to Hell Club." Not only did people survive, but also work sped up, as everyone felt empowered to focus on completing their jobs rather than be preoccupied with their own safety.

THE LEADERSHIP PARADOX

You might call this example a paradox. Suspending a safety net beneath a project costs both money and time. A leader might assume it's not worth the cost. Ironically, however, it saved time and money.

Similarly, life-giving leaders create an environment where team members are not afraid to fall, to falter or to fail. It's as though they place an imaginary "safety net" under the team. Suddenly, success comes more quickly because failure isn't final or fatal. The "net" empowers team members to succeed. They are concerned with doing the task well instead of simply surviving the job.

For several years now, our focus groups have informed us that today's young leaders have an extremely high fear of failure. In some ways, this is the fault of culture's message to young leaders: Whatever you do, don't make a mistake. Don't get it wrong. Don't fail. This may have left you with feelings of anxiety or the pressure to perform perfectly on every level.

A 2012 study posted in the *Journal of Experimental Psychology*, discovered this pressure might have a negative effect on learning. In several experiments, researchers found that students will perform self-protective acts and avoid any challenge where failure is an option. Another study found that anxiety disengages the prefrontal cortex, a region of the brain that plays an important role in flexible decision-making. We have trouble making good choices.[16] According to new studies published in *Educational Psychology*, "these students set the bar low, setting safe goals they're confident can be achieved. They're chronic underachievers."

Most leaders I know believe they have, indeed, created an environment where it's okay to make mistakes. Their team members, however, might say otherwise. My interviews reveal that too many students are absolutely horrified to do something wrong. They hold back by performing at below average levels, or they simply disengage. A 2015 report from *Gallup* shows 51 percent of the U.S. workforce is "not engaged" at work. I believe part of the reason is that people feel they have no "net" beneath them.[17] They don't want to fail so they don't do much at all.

What Could Your Team Look Like?

My guess is you've heard about organizations that practice the "Golden Gate Paradox" well. Years ago, I first heard of The 3M Company that not only encouraged risk taking, but they gave team members 15 percent of their week to experiment on projects they had dreamed up themselves. Chairman William McKnight would walk around, spotting employees working on unconventional ideas, and he would get excited about them, providing a sense of anticipation rather than anxiety. It paid off. Many of the products we use on a weekly basis were the result of this strategy: including Post-It Notes, masking tape, transparent tape, wet or dry waterproof sandpaper, and rubber cement. These were all created because the environment was life-giving and safe to make a mistake.

In *Habitudes for New Professionals*, I relay McKnight's basic rule of management:

> As our business grows, it becomes increasingly necessary to delegate responsibility and to encourage men and women to exercise their initiative. This requires considerable tolerance. Those men and women, to whom we delegate authority and responsibility, if they are good people, are going to want to do their jobs

in their own way. Mistakes will be made. But if a person is essentially right, the mistakes he or she makes are not as serious in the long run as the mistakes management will make if it undertakes to tell those in authority exactly how they must do their jobs. Management that is destructively critical when mistakes are made kills initiative. And it's essential that we have many people with initiative if we are to continue to grow.

Thomas J. Watson was a pioneer in computing equipment and built a global industry during his 42 years as CEO of IBM. Part of his legend was how easily he embraced mistakes. In the 1940s, an employee made a mistake that cost IBM a million dollars. Knowing he would likely be fired over it, the man quickly typed up his resignation letter and handed it to Watson. The CEO responded, "Fire you? I've just invested one million dollars in your education, and you think I'm going to fire you?"

What an attitude!

Working under John C. Maxwell for 20 years, I had this same experience. John would tell us, "A person must be big enough to admit his mistakes, smart enough to profit from them, and strong enough to correct them."

CREATING SAFETY NETS TO INSPIRE TEAMS

To create this kind of environment, try this leadership path:

1. Offer the gift of clarity
Make sure those you lead understand what a "win" looks like. At the end of a project, what is the specific outcome you're shooting for? What is the clear objective? Ensure everyone is on the same page. People must be aligned and energized by the target.

2. Extend the safety net principle
Let people know they have equal responsibility and authority to get their jobs done. Give them the freedom to try and make mistakes, while owning the project they are working on. Ultimately, they're free to fail, but must find a way to complete the task.

3. Practice "try it out and talk it over"
Team members feel safer to make mistakes and fail if they know they are free to try something new, record the results, and then meet with a leader to discuss the outcomes. As Jim Collins reminds us, "shoot bullets before cannon balls." Try out a small pilot project and see what hits the target before going big.

4. "Manage by walking around"
In this kind of environment, both creativity and mistakes will surface. You must be okay with both. You can minimize damage by practicing what Tom Peters calls MBWA: Manage by Walking Around—take a daily stroll to check out what's going on.

5. Recruit good people and trust the process

Once you get the right people in the right places on the team, do your best to trust the process you've created. While failure will happen, the price is worth it. Good things will be created and the benefit will outweigh the costs.

6. Ask the right questions to learn from mistakes

Instead of drawing conclusions or offering lectures, try leading with questions. Why did the mistake occur? Do they need more clarity and direction? Do they need extra support? Do they need the steps to be broken down? Be sure the questions communicate that you care and are confident in their abilities.

7. Express belief

This is the key action on your part. Be sure what you say and do relays belief in those you are leading. Discern what will communicate confidence, high expectations, and hope for them. Strong belief inspires strong behavior.

8. Follow through

Finally, whatever belief you've communicated, follow through in demonstrating its credibility. Don't undo what you've said with negativity or contradictory words. Be sure your actions match your words. This will help them "own" their work.

PLAYING THROUGH MISTAKES

Let me tell you about Roy "Wrong Way" Reigels. He was the NCAA football player who became famous when he picked up a fumble, and in his excitement, ran the wrong way toward the opposing team's end zone in the 1929 Rose Bowl. Roy was tackled by his own teammate, just before scoring for the other team. He got up, absolutely humiliated. He said later it was the worst day of his life.

What you may not know, is that during halftime, Coach Nibs Price said nothing about it. He gave an energizing pep talk and then said, "Alright, I want the same team to start the second half that started the first half."

Reigels couldn't believe it. In his disbelief, he just sat there, refusing to return to the field. With great discernment, Coach Price said to him as they sat alone in the locker room, "Roy, I believe in you. And, if you don't go out there and play this second half, everyone will remember you for what you just did in the first half. You owe it to yourself to show us all who you really are."

Coach Price said later that he'd never seen anyone play with more passion and intelligence than Roy Reigels did in that second half. He played through his mistake, but it took a life-giving leader with a safety net.

REFLECT AND RESPOND

1. What's the biggest reason why this principle is tough for people to practice?

_____

_____

2. What are the tangible benefits of a team that's empowered to make mistakes?

_____

_____

3. How can leaders balance freeing people to both make mistakes and make progress?

_____

_____

Assess Yourself

In raw honesty, place an X at the point on the line where you find yourself in your actions and emotions:

1. When I notice people making mistakes, I usually get preoccupied with…

|---|

OFFERING GRACE   **OFFERING CRITICISM**

2. As a leader, when things go wrong, I tend to…

|---|

BELIEVE THE BEST ABOUT PEOPLE   **SUSPECT THE WORST**

3. When I struggle with others failing on their tasks, it's usually because of…

|---|

THE LOSS OF PRODUCTIVITY   **HOW IT LOOKS TO OTHERS**

Try it Out: Practicing the Principle

This week, meet with your team and put some "safety nets" in place. Let others know it's okay to make mistakes on their projects. Then, follow through on the steps I offer in this chapter. Discuss the results by week's end. Was it a positive or negative week?

> *Life is the most difficult exam. Some people fail because they try to copy others not realizing everyone has a different question on their paper.* –Unknown

End Notes

REFEREES AND QUARTERBACKS

1. Jason Haber, "Why Millennials May Just Be the Best Entrepreneurial Generation Ever," Entrepreneur, June 16, 2016, https://www.entrepreneur.com/article/271972.

THREE BUCKETS

2. Yasmin Anwar, "Affluent People More Likely to be Scofflaws," Greater Good Magazine, February 28, 2012, https://greatergood.berkeley.edu/article/item/affluent_people_more_likely_to_be_scofflaws.

ROOT AND FRUIT

3. Stephen Covey, The 7 Habits of Highly Effective People, Coral Gables, FL: Mango Publishing Group, 1989.

4. iUeMagazine, "10 Warren Bennis Quotes on Leadership in Business," last modified June 3, 2017. http://www.iuemag.com/u17/di/10-warren-bennis-quotes-on-leadership-in-business.php.

SURGEONS AND VAMPIRES

5. Positive Parenting Ally, "Diana Baumrind's 3 Parenting Styles: Get a Full Understanding of the 3 Archetypical Parents," accessed June 6, 2018, https://www.positive-parenting-ally.com/3-parenting-styles.html.

6. Daniel Coyle, "The Simple Phrase that Increases Effort 40%," last modified December 13, 2013, http://danielcoyle.com/2013/12/13/the-simple-phrase-that-increases-effort-40/.

CLEAN WINDOWS

7. St. Thomas University, "What is Situational Leadership?" How Flexibility Leads to Success," last modified May 8, 2018, https://online.stu.edu/articles/education/what-is-situational-leadership.aspx.

SALUTES AND SNUBS

8. James A. Roberts and Meredith E. Davis, "My life has become a major distraction from my cell phone: Partner phubbing and relationship satisfaction among romantic partners," Computers in Human Behavior 54 (January 2016): 134-141, https://doi.org/10.1016/j.chb.2015.07.058.

9. Brainy Quote, "Laurence Sterne Quotes," accessed June 4, 2018, https://www.brainyquote.com/quotes/laurence_sterne_165818.

SPLASHES AND WAVES

10. Gerard R. Roche, "Much Ado About Mentors," Harvard Business Review, January 1979, https://hbr.org/1979/01/much-ado-about-mentors.

TEFLON AND VELCRO

11. Sparks & Honey, "Meet Generation Z: Forget Everything You Learned About Millennials," slideshow, last modified 2014, https://www.slideshare.net/sparksandhoney/generation-z-final-june-17.

FOUNTAINS AND DRAINS

12. Robert Emmons, "Why Gratitude is Good," Greater Good Magazine, November 16, 2010, https://greatergood.berkeley.edu/article/item/why_gratitude_is_good.

CULTURES AND CUSTOMS

13. TLF Research, "What's the Secret?" accessed June 4, 2018, https://www.tlfresearch.com/whats-the-secret/.

STETHOSCOPES AND TREATMENTS

14. Covey, 7 Habits.

15. Daniel Goleman, "Researchers Trace Empathy's Roots to Infancy," The New York Times, March 28, 1989, https://www.nytimes.com/1989/03/28/science/researchers-trace-empathy-s-roots-to-infancy.html.

THE GOLDENT GATE PARADOX

16. Frederique Autin and Jean-Claude Croizet, "Improving working memory efficiency by reframing metacognitive interpretation of task difficulty," Journal of Experimental Psychology: General 141, no. 4 (2012): 610-618, http://dx.doi.org/10.1037/a0027478.

17. Amy Adkins, "Employee Engagement in U.S. Stagnant in 2015," Gallup News, January 13, 2016, http://news.gallup.com/poll/188144/employee-engagement-stagnant-2015.aspx.

Acknowledgements

Allow me to acknowledge and thank the team of people who made this book possible. I am grateful for the gifted people who co-labored with me:

Andrew McPeak who oversaw the production of this book. His eye for excellence and attention to detail insure its message is clear.

Jim Woodard, who oversaw the layout and acquisition of the photographs. Jim understands what we're attempting to do as we teach and learn through images.

Emma Smith, who was our copy editor. She labors tirelessly to insure the grammar and spelling accurately relay the truths of this book.

Colin Eurit, who researched both data and stories for this book. Colin has become a servant leader in his own right.

Matt Litton, who served as our primary line editor, offering not only edits, but also wise counsel to insure the message of this book comes through loud and clear.

Chris Harris who drove our team to focus on what makes this book unique and how we might vividly describe its value to readers.

Holly Moore, who empowers our team to be life-giving leaders by modeling the way.

Notes

Notes

Notes

Notes

Notes

Enjoy Habitudes?

Help us bring these lessons to students who can't afford them.

1/4 Young Adults *live in* **POVERTY**

8/10 Young Adults *plan to* **MOVE HOME** *after College*

In both urban and rural environments, **students are sheltered** *within a 9-mile radius of their home,* **shielded from experiences** *that involve risk or failure.* **This leads to delayed maturity.**

All over the country and in developing nations around the world, there are students who are not equipped to lead themselves (or others) into the next steps of their lives. What's worse, their schools can't afford leadership development materials to help them mature into the best versions of themselves.

We want to change that. We want to help students broaden their vision, take bigger risks, think bigger thoughts, and pursue bigger goals.

To do this, we created **The Growing Leaders Initiative,** to provide *Habitudes* in schools and youth non-profit organizations that cannot afford to purchase programs for their students. Thanks to donor support, grants are available for qualified applicants.

To apply or donate, visit www.TheGrowingLeadersInitiative.com.

The **GROWING LEADERS** Initiative